the SUPER simple guide to KOI

Brian M. Scott

t.f.h.

T.F.H. Publications, Inc.

Distributed in the UNITED STATES to the Pet Trade by T.F.H. Publications, Inc., 1 TFH Plaza, Neptune City, NJ 07753; on the Internet at www.tfh.com; in CANADA by Rolf C. Hagen Inc., 3225 Sartelon St., Montreal, Quebec H4R 1E8; Pet Trade by H & L Pet Supplies Inc., 27 Kingston Crescent, Kitchener, Ontario N2B 2T6; in ENGLAND by T.F.H. Publications, PO Box 74, Havant PO9 5TT; in AUSTRALIA AND THE SOUTH PACIFIC by T.F.H. (Australia), Pty. Ltd., Box 149, Brookvale 2100 N.S.W., Australia; in NEW ZEALAND by Brooklands Aquarium Ltd., 5 McGiven Drive, New Plymouth, RD1 New Zealand; in SOUTH AFRICA by Rolf C. Hagen S.A. (PTY.) LTD., P.O. Box 201199, Durban North 4016, South Africa; in Japan by T.F.H. Publications. Published by T.F.H. Publications, Inc.

Library of Congress Cataloging-in-Publication Data
Scott, Brian M.
The super simple guide to koi / Brian M. Scott.
p. cm.
Includes index.
ISBN 0-7938-3450-3 1. Koi. I. Title.
SF458.K64S36 2003
639.3'7483--dc22
2003018413

Contents

Origins of Koi

Understanding Water Quality

Dedication

This book is dedicated to my wonderful mother, Carol. If it were not for her, none of this would have been possible.

Acknowledgements

The author would like to acknowledge the following individuals for their assistance in the production of this book: Carol and Rick Stevens, Ginny and Steve Zudnak, Robert and Michelle Capri, the staff of Pet Agree Pet Supplies, Pat Grady and the rest of the staff at Water World, and finally, Lisa, for putting up with the seemingly endless hours of writing that this project required.

Part One
Understanding Koi

Origin and Natural History of Koi

Early records of koi keeping date back more than 2,500 years in Asia, but the farm cultivation of koi is considerably more recent. Color mutations that have given rise to modern varieties only trace back to about 200 years or so, and many didn't come about until even later. These color mutations and modern varieties are due to the

Koi are direct descendents of the common carp, *Cyprinus carpio*.

This is a grand champion taisho sanke, showing a near perfect red/black distribution.

dedication of fish farmers worldwide and their passion for producing new and different strains of koi for the hobby.

The 20th century brought about new explorations in travel, completely expanding the koi hobby. While the use of road and rail links played a huge role in the advancement of koi keeping, no other mode of transportation has revolutionized the koi industry as much as the airplane. With this rise in industry and motorized travel, koi began to find their way across Asia and then across the world.

Now koi farms have been started in many countries, and although the finest koi are said to be found in Japan, countries such as Great Britain, Hong Kong, and Israel are producing very high-quality koi of their own. German koi fanciers are also producing top-quality fish. The patience of the German hobbyists closely resembles the disciplined techniques of the Japanese, and, in time, hobbyists should see many fine examples being offered by German aquarists.

What Are Koi?

The name, Koi, is short for the Japanese name of "Nishikigoi." Koi are colored descendants of the somewhat bland-colored common carp, *Cyprinus carpio*, or Magoi as they were known in Japan. Magoi is a dark-colored koi (usually exhibiting an orange belly), and it is Japanese custom to have one in your fishpond, as they are believed to bring good luck and health. Often, the name "Japanese Colored Carp" is also applied to these magnificent fish because koi are, in fact, still carp scientifically speaking. However, they have been selectively bred for many years to show their unique and often dramatic colorations and patterns.

There is certainly no shortage of the varieties of koi that are available today. One of the most popular "styles" of koi is the Kohaku. Kohaku have a red on white coloration, producing a bold contrast that is easily seen from above. Koi have many color, fin, and scale variations, which will be discussed in more detail later in this book. For now, we will concentrate on the understanding the koi and what makes them different and unique when compared with the many thousands of other species of fishes worldwide.

Developing a Plan

Now that you have decided to attempt keeping koi in your garden pond, you should begin to plan what you ultimately want to achieve. Whether it is the successful reproduction of koi, raising young koi for resale, or simply just having a few good-looking, large

Where Do Carp Originate?

Carp are native to Eurasia and the Middle East, where they thrive in cool-water rivers, lakes, and streams. Over many years, it became apparent that carp had a commercial value both as a sport fish and a food fish. The Japanese then took their commercialization one step further once they recognized that these fish could have their appearances altered in such a way as to provide a somewhat colorful fish to inhabit the fishponds in their water gardens.

First introduced to North America in 1831 as a game fish, carp are now widely distributed, covering many states and most commonly found in muddy, man-made bodies of water that are high in organic matter. They feed mainly on sedimentary organisms, such as insects, larvae, worms, and other invertebrates, for which they search out using their terminal mouths and sensitive barbells. It is not uncommon to see several large adults swimming calmly together through the aquatic vegetation and underwater roots and tangles. They often inhabit very shallow water that hardly covers their backs. This makes them easy targets for spear fishermen and trappers alike.

Carp can reach lengths of 40 inches or more, making them one of the largest freshwater fishes in North America. They are robust fish with a hearty appetite, and adult carp have few natural predators. This, combined with their highly successful reproductive manner, allows them to produce many young each year. Over much of their range, both natural and introduced, juvenile carp are a very important forage fish for predators such as pike, *Esox*; Bass, *Micropterus*; and sunfishes, *Lepomis*.

fish in your backyard garden pond, there should be a plan to keep your goal focused.

The success of your endeavor will depend on many factors, such as space, money, time, quality of stock available to you, and so on.

However, one factor supercedes the rest–information. You must be informed on all aspects of koi keeping in order to be successful in your efforts and to get the most enjoyment out of your hobby.

The Importance of Information

Never underestimate the power of exchanging information. One of the most important steps a new hobbyist interested in koi should take is research; read whatever material you can get a hold of.

Hobbyists have a vast assortment of resources at their disposal regarding koi and how to care for them. There are many great books on the market and several magazine publications. Often, koi clubs publish a newsletter or journal, usually bi-monthly, on the latest news of color strains, equipment, and husbandry practices and techniques. It is highly recommended that you look into one of these clubs, perhaps the one closest to your home. As you become more advanced in this hobby, you will find yourself joining several of these clubs and going to their

You will need a well thought-out plan in order to raise a fish like this sanke to adulthood.

meetings as often as possible. Koi keeping is one of the few healthy addictions!

Showing Off Your Koi

Koi clubs are found worldwide. The first official exhibitions where people gathered to show off their koi are thought to have taken place in Japan in the early 1900s. Often, prize-winning koi command very respectable prices if their owners choose to sell them. In fact, it is not unusual for very high-quality koi to sell for higher prices than most new homes.

Outside of Japan, many koi clubs hold annual shows or exhibitions where hobbyists and professionals alike have a chance to gather and swap information and ideas to improve their koi-keeping experience. These meetings are becoming more popular as the popularity and affordability of garden ponds increase. Of course, these meetings have positive influences on beginners who look up to their peers when beginning a new adventure in the art of pond keeping.

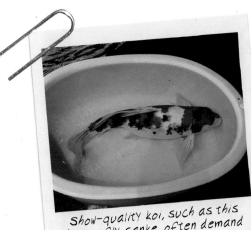

Show-quality koi, such as this butterfly sanke, often demand huge prices.

The Japanese recognize 195 basic classes comprising 13 varieties of koi in 15 different size groups. Within these groups, there are further divisions, and thus the potential for mutations adds up very quickly. In the future, more size groups will be constructed, as the potential maximum size for koi is a staggering 4 feet in total length (TL). Koi of that size will undoubtedly make today's jumbo size group look like common goldfish! Koi of this size are certainly a possibility. However, they are limited by genetics, foods, feeding practices, rearing, and environmental conditions. As better feeding and rearing methods are being developed, we should see fish of this size class begin making their way into koi collector circles worldwide.

Here is another sanke, showing many excellent attributes that make this strain one of the most popular with hobbyists.

Anatomy and Physiology of Koi

It is vital for the long-term health of your fishes and your hobby to understand some basic principles of anatomy, physiology, and behavior of your prized koi. The following information should serve as a general guide or as a quick reference.

The anatomy of koi, and many other fishes, is very basic.

This koi shows the basic fusiform shape that koi exhibit.

Part 1

Certainly, there are fishes that exhibit very complicated and intricate anatomy and associated physiology, but those fishes are not often available to hobbyists and are beyond the scope of this book. On the other hand, koi have evolved to survive in a wide variety of habitats and remain very similar in appearance and function to their wild cousins, the carp. The only major differences are fin size and body coloration.

Figuring out what strain of koi you have is sometimes difficult.

Internal Anatomy and Physiology

Certainly the internal anatomy of koi is far more advanced in comparison to the external anatomy. This is true not only due to the organs involved, but also because of the functions in which these organs perform. Just as in humans, koi have circulatory, nervous, skeletal, and reproductive systems. Because koi are vertebrates, meaning they have a backbone, the function of these systems is remarkably similar to other vertebrates, such as birds, reptiles, and even humans.

One distinct difference between koi and many other vertebrates is that koi, like most fishes, are cold-blooded. This means that koi have

Part 1

a body temperature that is not internally regulated but adjusts to approximately the same as the outside environment. Therefore, koi will move into shallow water to warm up when the water is cool, then into deeper water as the water temperature increases. Koi may move back and forth between deep and shallow water several times each day as the outside environment dictates.

As the water depth increases, the water temperature has a tendency to remain more constant. Usually koi will show signs of dormancy when the water temperature falls below 55 F. However, it is more likely that the dormancy of koi is triggered by decreasing hours of daylight rather than water temperature.

This is an exceptionally large kohaku, showing near-perfect coloration.

One feature of the internal anatomy of koi that should be described in detail is the swim bladder. Sometimes called the gas bladder, the swim bladder is responsible for the buoyancy of the fish as it moves in water. It is an elongated oval sac that lies just anterior to the vertebral column.

The swim bladder is pinched at the forward end, resulting in a narrow constriction. Here there is a duct that connects the swim bladder to the gut, where air that is gulped at the surface can bleed into the swim bladder, allowing maximum buoyancy. As the air inside the swim bladder is diffused into the bloodstream, the koi will make periodic charges to the surface to gulp more air to "top off" its swim bladder. It is important to understand this area of anatomy, as koi often suffer from infections of the swim bladder. Having an understanding of its function may help you help your fish later on.

Scale arrangement is very important in koi. An asagi is pictured here.

External Anatomy and Physiology

A fish's external anatomy consists of several important features: scales, fins, lateral line system, eyes, and mouth. All of these features work together to perform several key functions, such as feeding, breeding, and locomotion.

The scales of a fish serve as protection against abrasive objects and the elements. Fishes such as koi inhabit mainly shallow water, where they come in contact with rocks, roots, and fallen trees. These and many other objects would normally injure them if they did not have scales to protect their delicate skin.

Part 1

Covering the scales is a thin coat of mucus often referred to as the "slime coat." This layer of mucus is mildly antiseptic and is secreted by special cells within the dermis of the koi's skin. Not only does the slime coat allow objects to glide off the fish, but it also provides very effective lubri-cation, which, in turn, allows the koi to be even more hydrodynamic in the water.

The fins of koi are larger than those of carp and often are very elegant. They serve as stabilizers and are responsible for the propulsion of the fish through water. Koi have two sets of paired fins, the pelvic (ventral) fins and the pectoral fins. The pelvic fins are located on the ventral surface (bottom) approximately mid-body. These are the main fins used for directional changes and for ascending and descending as the fish propels itself through the water.

The pectoral fins on the koi are located just posterior to the gill operculum and are responsible for braking. They are also used for rotation as the fish hovers over the substrate searching for food. Some suggest that the pectoral fins of bottom feeding fishes such as koi are used to fan the substrate to

The pectoral fins on this bekko appear small but still play a very important role in stabilization.

uncover possible foodstuffs that lie just under the uppermost sedimentary layers in shallow waters.

The remaining three fins on the koi are unpaired, meaning they do not posses another of the same type to act with or against it. Of these three fins, none are more or less important than the next. They are all responsible for their own individual functions.

First, the dorsal fin's major job is the stability of the fish in the water column. It serves a similar function to a keel on a ship and allows the koi to remain upright in all but the most turbid of waters. When the fish wants to move away rapidly, it simply lowers the dorsal fin and kicks off with its caudal fin.

Secondly, the caudal fin of a koi is responsible for its forward movement. It attains maximum thrust due to its surface-to-water area and forked shape, which allows minimum drag. Fish exhibiting a forked caudal fin are usually known for their speed capabilities. Certainly koi do not swim rapidly all of the time, but when they have a need for speed, the fins they have developed allow them to move at a very rapid pace.

Finally, the anal fin of koi works as a counter-stabilizer to the dorsal fin. Although this and the dorsal fin are not considered paired fins, they do work with one another to serve as an overall stabilizer for the fish. This is especially important in faster-flowing waters, where the need for stability is greatest.

Part 1

The Unique Features of Koi

Koi do not possess anything that other fishes do not. However, they do exhibit some very unique features when compared to other fishes within their family. These features are not only anatomical but are also behavioral.

In regard to their anatomy, koi have two pairs of barbels, one pair on either side of the mouth. These structures are covered in taste buds that allow the koi to taste whatever the barbels come in contact with. The barbels are used to find grubs, insect larvae, crustaceans, worms, and other tasty edibles in the substrate.

Another unique feature of the koi's anatomy is the mouth. As juveniles, koi have what is termed as a terminal mouth. A terminal mouth is defined as a mouth that is pointed downward and used for feeding off of the bottom. As koi grow and mature, their mouths develop into sub-terminal mouths, meaning they turn only slightly in a terminal fashion.

This development suggests a transition in feeding strategy and possibly a dietary change as the fish grow larger. Some biologists speculate that sub-adult and adult

The most unique feature of koi is their behavior.

koi have a higher percentage of plant matter found in their gut than juvenile specimens. If this transition is valid, then it may explain why their mouths develop from terminal to sub- terminal; a down-turned mouth would be less necessary for grazing on aquatic vegetation.

From a behavioral viewpoint, koi are among the most "social" of fishes. Their ability to recognize their owner from other humans is second to none. It is not uncommon for koi to actively come to the surface when their favorite human comes to the pond, but when another person walks over, the koi ignore his or her presence altogether. Certainly koi are not the only fish that exhibit this behavior, but they are definitely within a special clad of them. It is also important to mention that koi live very long. It is not uncommon for koi to survive more than 30 years, and the social bonds that are made are also long-lived.

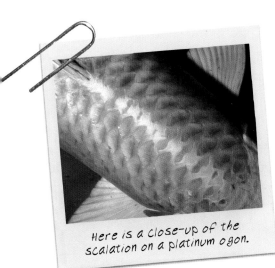

Here is a close-up of the scalation on a platinum ogon.

Part Two
Diving into Koi

"oh-oh."

The Selection Process

When the time comes to purchase your koi, you should be able to determine which fish to buy and which to stay away from. If you are an experienced fish collector, this area should not give you a problem. However, if you have never purchased a koi before (and many of you probably have not), then you should pay

With so many colors to choose from, selecting your koi can be quite a task.

special attention to the information provided in this chapter. There is little worse than getting home with your new and sometimes very expensive addition for your pond and realizing it has a disease or disorder.

Knowing What to Look For

The purchase of a new fish can be a very exciting day for the whole family to share. Koi are not just any normal fish; they are often considered family members because of their keen abilities for owner recognition and their tendency to "beg" for attention and food. It is not uncommon for people to spend hours or even days in search of the new addition to their koi collection.

Often, advanced hobbyists will request that their dealer hold their fish for several days or weeks so the potential owners can see what type of personality the fish may exhibit. It is also common for advanced koi buyers to put deposits on several fish at one time only to select one or two fish in the end. This may sound a bit extreme, but when you're spending several thousand dollars for a champion grade bloodline, a few hundred dollars more really is not too steep a price to ensure you are getting the friendliest and healthiest fish you possibly can.

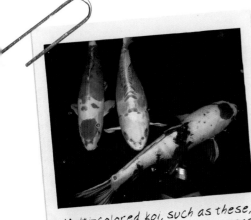

Multi-colored koi, such as these, are very popular with koi keepers.

Behavior

A healthy koi will normally do one of two things when you approach the holding pool: it will either swim away at a steady pace or greet you and beg for food. In a nutshell, you should avoid koi that are listless and sit on the bottom, as they are commonly suffering from internal bacterial or fungal infections, or they have been subjected to improper water conditions and are experiencing ammonia toxicity.

Ammonia toxicity is common in newly imported specimens where their flight may have been delayed or canceled, and they were required to sit in their transport bags for extended periods of time. Koi that have been through this trauma are often in shock and may take several days to adjust to their new holding pools. Sadly, if they have been exposed to very heavy ammonia concentrations in their transports bags, there may be irreversible damage to their gills, eyes, and fins. Consequently the koi will suffer a slow, painful death.

The yellow-colored koi, shown here, are fairly new to the koi scene.

Gill Damage

A good way to tell if the fish you are picking from have gill damage is to notice their breathing or pumping rates. Often, koi that have gill damage will pump their gills at a rapid pace, appearing as if they cannot get oxygenated water over them quickly enough. From time to time, you will notice a series of very rapid pulsing motions of the gills. These are signs that the gill membranes have excessive mucus on them, possibly from a parasite but more commonly from damage due to ammonia toxicity. There are a few treatments you can try in order to save the fish's life, and these will be covered in greater detail later on in the book.

Eye Damage

Koi have very sensitive eyes that do not react well to transport. Often, koi that are in shock will initially swim very rapidly throughout their acclimating containers and, consequently, rub their eyes along the sides. This causes the corneas of the eyes to cloud over and subjects them to further infection. You should steer clear of such specimens and maybe even point out those that exhibit this to the handlers. If left untreated, the eyes will begin to cave inward, due to an internal fungal infection, and the fish will become blind in one or both eyes. Sadly, beautiful koi often exhibit poor eye quality due to improper handling at some point in their lives.

Fin Damage

When compared to gill and eye damage, fin damage is usually much more treatable with little or no permanent damage to the koi. When fin damage is the result of high ammonia, it is referred to as "ammonia burn." Fins that have suffered ammonia burn will usually heal completely; however, if the fins have degenerated far enough to where the fin meets the body, there may be irreversible damage and they may never regenerate. If they do grow back, often they will be deformed. The very first few centimeters of the fish's fins are usually going to show a little ammonia burn, especially during the first 24 to 36 hours after arrival. The dead fin tissue will fall off and heal over in the next few days. New fin growth should appear almost immediately.

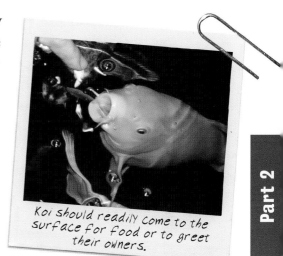

Koi should readily come to the surface for food or to greet their owners.

Split fins are another issue with koi. During transport, koi will often bang into each other in their fruitless efforts to get out of the transports bags. This may result in fin tears and splits. Similar to ammonia-burned fins, these wounds will also heal completely unless the damage extends to the fin/body junction. Again, many absolutely stunning koi have unsightly fin damage that all but ruins their chances for exhibition in shows, but that does not stop them from being wonderful pets, of course.

Looking into a pool full of koi shows you just how many varieties there are.

Part 2

Basic Varieties of Koi

Now that you know what constitutes a healthy specimen as compared to a less healthy specimen, you can focus on size, pattern, and coloration of the koi you wish to add to your garden pond. While the Japanese accept up to 17 basic varieties, the Americans and British accept only as many as 13. It is fair to state that this is a very dynamic area in koi keeping and one that is argued to no end each year by many serious koi enthusiasts.

Brilliant red markings, as exhibited by this kohaku, indicate a very high-quality fish.

In each of the basic varieties, there are many different color and pattern forms. Certainly a comprehensive overview of this area is out of the scope of this book. However, the following section will provide you with a brief description of these color and pattern forms.

Kohaku

This was the first color variety, established and perfected by the Japanese in the early 19th century. It is a white fish with overlying red patterns in various shapes and sizes. Only red on white is acceptable. If there are any other colors present on the fish, it will be disqualified as a pure Kohaku immediately. Of course, as with all koi, the body shape, fin size, and appearance must first be of superior quality before color and pattern can be focused on.

Good-quality Kohaku colored koi must have brilliant red markings, known as Hi by the Japanese. In show fish, these markings should not extend past the nostrils, lateral line, or any of the fins. The edges should remain uniform and sharp, not faded or blended. The most important thing to keep in mind when shopping for Kohaku koi is the even distribution and intensity of the Hi.

Taisho Sanke

The first Taisho Sanke colored koi are thought to have appeared in the late 1800s to early 1900s. It is thought that this color variety was a product of Kohaku koi and Magoi (black) koi being bred together to get a tri-colored fish. This fish normally has only a small amount of black pigmentation, or Sumi, spread over the body, but it is favorable to have a large patch of Sumi on the shoulder. The Sumi should never appear on the head of the Taisho Sanke that are being considered for exhibition.

The sanke is one of the most popular color varieties of modern koi available to hobbyists

Showa Sanke

The Taisho era ended in 1927 with the rise of the Showa Sanke colored koi. The Showa Sanke is a black koi that has Hi and white color imposed over the body. This is a color variant that was developed by a famous Japanese koi breeder named Jukichi Hoshino. He bred a Kohaku and a Ki-Utsuri to develop this strain, which was further refined over many more years. The end result was a color variant that is now considered one of the "big three" in Japan.

Utsuri Mono

This fish is Motogura, having a black base with only one other color. The second color is most often white, but it is acceptable to have yellow or red. Bright yellow and black specimens are becoming more common and are cherished in the Western areas of the world. This variant of koi is an older type dating back to the Meji era (1862-1912) in its Ki form, or yellow form. There are no records indicating when other color variants were achieved.

Bekko

The Bekko is a black on a colored background fish. Most commonly pure white is the base for which the

Bekko, such as this one, are of superior quality and are usually hard to find.

Sumi is imposed. More commonly, Bekko colored koi have a dirty appearance. There are conflicting thoughts as to why, but generally it can be agreed upon that it is genetics from past sources that gave rise to the Bekko color in the first place. Perhaps dedicated koi enthusiasts will develop more pure white with Sumi in the future.

Asagi-Shusui

These are actually two fishes that are grouped as one because the Shusui was produced from the Asagi. The Asagi is an old color of koi that is thought to be one of the first color variants separated from the original Nishikigoi. It is regarded as a mutant of an older the mutant, the black koi or Magoi. There are as many as nine varieties of the Asagi-Shusui classification, and some are recognized more than others.

Koromo

This color variant of koi is considered a hybrid. You can achieve this by breeding an Asagi to a Kohaku, Taisho, or Showa Sanke. The Japanese meaning for this variant is "robed," so if you place an Asagi pattern over a Showa Sanke, you will end up with a Koromo. This is only one

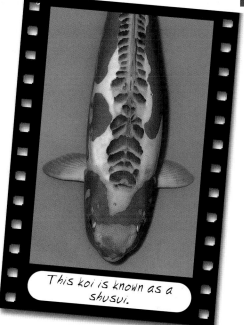

This koi is known as a shusui.

The kohaku is the starting point to developing the koromo.

of many so-called hybrids regarding Japanese koi varieties, but the Koromo seems to be one of the more popular ones. This is most likely due to the ability to recognize a distinct pattern of another type of fish under the robed appearance.

Kawarimono

This is a group comprised of oddball koi varieties. Many of these varieties are remarkably similar to more traditional varieties, but they may show a slight variation that is enough to reclassify them in this category. The Japanese have their explanations for this, and most seem logical. However there are many fish in this clad that could be further lumped together but, for unknown reasons, have not been so far.

Ogon

The Japanese term for gold is "Ogon." While the Japanese refer to Ogon in the strict sense of meaning solid gold, Americans often refer to Ogon as meaning either solid gold or silver. Often, you will see names such as Platinum Ogon assigned to koi that are white with silver reticulation on their scales, giving them an almost mother-of-pearl appearance. Another common name for these koi is Hikari-mujimono. If this fish is an Ogon, then we say it is the "shiny golden one."

Hikari Utsuri

This variation is made up of several bloodlines. The fish is Hikari, or shiny, but it also includes crosses of Ogons, both types of Utsuri, and even some Showa Sanke as well. Apparently the Hi has an annoying tendency to fade to an orange color, reducing the quality drastically. It can, however, produce some interesting shades of brown, and the fish obviously still make fantastic pets.

The lemon drop, or gold ogon, is a very popular koi in the US.

Part 2

Kinginrin

This is a shiny-scaled koi that has been bred showing almost every other known variant out there. These fish appear to have a gold and silver glitter dusted all over their bodies, and when they are in direct sunlight, they exhibit one of the most striking scale patterns

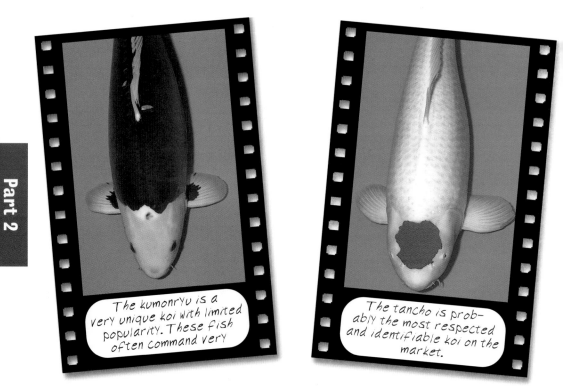

The kumonryu is a very unique koi with limited popularity. These fish often command very

The tancho is probably the most respected and identifiable koi on the market.

available. There are four classifications that koi may fall into with Kinginrin coloration: Kado, Tama, Hiroshima, and Beta.

Tancho

Finally, we have the awesome Tancho. The best-quality Tancho are those that exhibit a snow-white body with no imperfections and a bright circular Hi centered perfectly on the top of the head. These koi are named after the Manchurian crane, which sports a round or oval patch of red on the top of its head.

Buying Your Koi

Now that you have a good idea of what to look for in healthy specimens of the different basic varieties of koi, you can begin to shop around for your new addition. As you now know, there is a huge assortment of Japanese koi varieties, and there are even more varieties from other countries like Vietnam, Israel, Germany, and China, so you should be able to find something that suits your fancy.

It is not uncommon for experienced koi buyers to have their fish held for several days or weeks in order to be certain that their fish is in optimum condition before being transported to their final destination. Often, you will arrive at a koi retailer only to have a crowd of people standing there and closely examining a shipment of new arrivals. This is the best time to be at a koi retailer, as you can get a good idea as to what others are looking for. You may even be able to work out trades or barters with the retailer and some of his or her loyal customers.

Many people are rather impatient when purchasing their new koi and rush into things. This is not always a bad thing, but it should be avoided whenever possible. If you have a large pond and few or no other fish, then a quick buy will most likely not do any damage. However, if you have a pond full of prized pets, then an impulsive purchase may mean certain death to your entire collection. Even if you rush into a purchase, never add the koi to your collection without a quarantine period of at least one week.

YOU should never purchase a koi if it:

- Does not eat
- Sways from side to side
- Shows red blemishes on it's fins or body
- Possesses split or torn fins
- Appears emaciated

Adjusting Your Fish to Their New Home

Well, the big day is here, and it is time to bring home a new koi. Ideally, your fish has been at the retailer's for at least a few days and is eating in a healthy way. Your retailer will know not to feed your fish for 24 hours prior to pickup as to minimize the amount of waste that your fish will excrete in its transport container or bag. Small and medium koi will usually be placed in plastic bags, while large and jumbo specimens will require containers, such as totes or buckets, to effectively transport them in a safe and secure manner.

Once you have gone to the retailer and picked up the fish, you will want to drive straight home, making as few stops (preferably none) as you can. You do not want the fish in the holding bag for any longer than it has to be. Once you arrive home, immediately open the bag and allow fresh air to hit the water's surface. Now you can dump the contents of the bag and the fish into a larger container, so the new koi can be acclimated properly.

Once the fish is in this holding container, you may begin to adjust the fish to its new home. If the fish has been at the retailer's shop

The most effective and least stressful method of acclimatizing your fish to their new home is as follows.

1. Place the fish in a large, shallow container with all the transport water.

2. Remove some of the transport water until it slightly exposes the back of the koi.

3. Using a piece of airline tubing, begin to siphon water from the main pond into the holding container. (You may tie a loose knot in the tubing to adjust the water flow.)

4. Let the water siphon into the holding container until there is approximately twice the volume of water you started with.

5. Stop the siphon and remove the volume of water needed to slightly expose the fish's back again.

6. Repeat steps 3 and 4 at least two more times in order to ensure that the majority of the old water has been removed.

7. Allow the koi to sit in the container with the majority of new pond water for another 10 to 15 minutes.

8. Carefully remove the koi using a koi sock or container and quickly place in the new pond.

Part 2

for more than a few weeks, you usually will not have to quarantine the fish, as it should be devoid of any parasites or bacterial/fungal infections. When in doubt, however, always quarantine them for at least a week just to be sure. Tips and techniques for quarantining your new arrivals can be found later in the book.

Your koi usually will adjust quickly to their new home. In no time, they should be up and moving about.

You can add a drop or two of methylene blue to the transport water to give it a blue tint. This will allow you to see just how much old water remains after the acclimation process has been completed.

There are many variations to the above method for acclimatizing fishes. Most retailers are extremely knowledgeable in this practice and can instruct you further if you are having difficulties. Never settle for one method only. Instead, as you become experienced, try creating a hybrid of several different methods and devise a plan of your own.

Nutritional Requirements

Koi are considered omnivores due to the fact that they consume both animal and plant materials to obtain a wide assortment of protein, minerals, and vitamins for use in reproduction and survival. Unlike goldfish, koi have very specific dietary requirements that must be met in order to achieve maximum growth,

Feeding your koi should be enjoyable.

color, and reproductive success. The reason koi are being compared to goldfish in this chapter is because goldfish and koi diets are often treated very much the same. This is huge mistake, and it would not take a long time to see the negative effects that a goldfish diet would have on a high-quality koi. You will see foods labeled "for all pondfish" or "goldfish and koi," but these products should raise red flags when you are shopping around for different foods for your prized koi.

Foods & Feeding

The types of foods and frequency of feeding should be well thought-out and regimented to ensure the proper growth and development of your koi. Koi, like dogs, will usually eat continuously, and their appetites never seem to be satisfied.

This kohaku is a product of frequent feedings of good-quality foods.

This can be a problem, especially if you have young children who like nothing better than to sit on the edge of the pond and throw handful after handful of food into it.

If this happens, you can bet on one of two things happening: either the fish will die because of overfeeding, or the fish will die because the excessive food will cause the pond to become a cesspool. Therefore, it is necessary to carefully regulate the types of food you give your koi and how often you feed them.

Prepared Diets

Prepared diets are food products that are ready for immediate feeding; they are the most common type and the easiest to handle. These are considered to be the fast foods of the fish world because they often contain a lot of ingredients that the fish do not need but taste great or have specific uses such as fillers, binders, and so on. Koi and many other pondfishes usually take to these foods very quickly but usually suffer the consequences from them as well.

Prepared foods do, in fact, have their place in the proper care and well-being of koi. However, the trick is to feed a highly varied diet consisting of several types of prepared feeds in conjunction with live and fresh foods. Many Japanese koi owners use a wide assortment of these prepared feeds and find them to be the easiest way to deliver stabilized alpha and beta-carotenes to their fish. These feeds are considered to be "color enhancing" or, if your fishes are already vibrant, they are referred to as "color stabilizing" feeds.

Competition can be fierce at feeding time, so make sure each fish gets its fair share.

Part 2

Prepared foods come in a vast assortment of shapes and sizes, the most common being pellet feed, due to its buoyancy and convenience. Food pellets also come in a sinking form, which allows you to offer food to new arrivals that are not yet accustomed to rising to the surface to feed or to other fishes that are bottom-feeders, such as catfishes and suckers. Pellet feeds come in various sizes, so koi of all sizes can be accommodated.

Another common form of prepared food is "flaked food," which is made as a paste that is baked in large sheets, cooled, and then broken up into large flakes. Flaked food is a commonly used to feed young or newly imported koi. Flaked foods often float initially and then sink when waterlogged. Most flaked foods begin to sink approximately 30 to 40 seconds after being added to the water, depending on the size and density of the flakes. This can allow enough time for skittish koi to examine the food on the surface and then wait for the food to begin to sink so it can be consumed.

After several feedings, the koi will usually begin to meet the flakes halfway down the water column. Eventually, they will rise to the surface and feed as soon as the flakes are added. These are the first steps in a method we call "surface training." This method will be discussed in greater detail later on in this chapter.

Fresh Foods

One of the biggest misconceptions regarding koi diets is the use of fresh foods. What are fresh foods? Basically, fresh foods are any assortment of foods that have not been freeze-dried, frozen, or preserved in any direct way.

There are a wide variety of foods available to your koi that fall into this category. First and foremost is the use of fresh fruits and vegetables. Koi, especially large koi, relish the use of grapes and pieces of bananas in their diets periodically. Feel free to

Koi such as this require fresh foods in order to keep their brilliance.

try various other fruits as well, such as apples, pears, mangos, raspberries, and peaches. Once you discover which of these fresh foods your koi like, offer them foods in very small pieces. However, remember that these foods are **not** to be used as a staple diet but as an additive to their staple diet.

Certain fresh foods that have been used for years with many pondfish really should not be considered for use with koi. Some of these include but are not limited to rice, corn, bread, peanuts, and birdseeds. None of the mentioned foods are actually bad for the koi on a nutritional level, but they may cause harm with a koi's digestive system. Bread-based foods and rice will swell when exposed to water and can cause a major blockage, leading to constipation and sometimes death. Koi basically cannot digest corn at all, and corn can cause a major blockage if fed excessively. Peanuts and other seeds affect koi in a similar way.

Live Foods

With koi, the use of live foods is mainly restricted to feeder fishes, such as fathead minnows, goldfish, or young livebearers like swordtails or mollies. Feeding your koi live fishes is a great way to enhance the coloration of your koi and maintain vigor. Koi love to chase down the small fish, and it offers them a little exercise as well.

Insects are another type of live food for a koi's diet. Because insects are attracted to koi ponds, they can be considered a natural food item. If your koi pond has a lot of trees or shrubs around it, you will most likely have a good population of worms beneath the soil's surface, especially during steady rains, when you may find several dozen of these at a time.

Live foods, such as guppies or minnows, also provide something for the koi to chase.

Your fish will often go in a feeding frenzy if you throw a small handful of worms in the pond. Remember, koi are bottom-feeders by nature, so they have a terminal mouth and this helps them suck up the worms off the bottom of the pond. Wild carp often search out aquatic worms in the submerged vegetation, so koi have an instinctual taste for these insects. Worms are also great reward treats to give your koi when they do something you want them to do, such as greet you or allow you to pet them. Treats allow you to build a trusting bond with your koi, and this bond can last a lifetime.

These koi have been offered good food for a long time and nearly jump out of the water during feeding time.

Part 2

There are several other insects that also make great koi food. Mealworms, wax worms, bloodworms (midge larvae), black worms, tubifex worms, and soft-shelled crickets are some good examples. Feed insects sparingly and never feed them to your koi if you cannot guarantee that they have been collected or grown in a pesticide-free environment. Also, stay away from insects that have the ability to sting, such as bees, wasps, and biting flies. The toxins can build up and kill your koi or other pondfishes. Also stay away from fireflies–the chemicals that cause them to glow or bio-illuminate are also toxic and may kill your koi if they are ingested.

From Fry to Adults

As koi grow from young fry into adulthood, they require huge amounts of food, space, and water. Food is probably considered to

be the most important of these
requirements, however. This is
because space and water quality can
be altered with a large turnover rate in
man-made systems, such as pools and
aquariums. Food, on the other hand,
has to remain of good quality and
carry a balanced ratio of nutrients in
order to sustain koi and allow them to
grow to their potential.

Feed your fish small amounts of food frequently rather than large amounts of food sporadically.

Koi also need to have good genetics. Certainly, all of the varieties
have individual specimens that will grow to their optimum
standards, but some varieties are likely to produce more fish that
are of sound genetics than others. You will be able to determine
which variety suits your likes/dislikes when the time comes to
purchase yours.

Feeding Koi Fry

When koi hatch out of their protective eggs, they are so tiny that
they are barely visible. At this stage, they are eating microscopic
foods called infusoria. These foodstuffs are found naturally in pond
water and are comprised of many species of microscopic plants and
animals. They are often considered freshwater "plankton." Koi fry
feed constantly and should never be without food. They grow very
rapidly, often attaining some coloration in less than two or three
weeks if the right amount of proper food has been given to them.

If you are lucky enough to hatch out your own koi fry from adults that have spawned in your pond, then you will have to do one of two things. One option is to leave the fry in the pond in the hopes that some will make it to a size where they are no longer considered food by their pond mates. This is a good idea if you have never raised baby fishes before because koi are not the easiest fish to rear to adulthood. If you have a lot of submerged vegetation in your pond, you will likely have satisfactory results, because the vegetation offers koi fry a safe haven from many predators and offers them a good source of food as well.

The second option is to gently scoop or siphon out the koi fry when you see them beginning to appear from their eggs. You should place them in a container with water from the main pond and prevent any quick changes in their environment, such as temperature and water chemistry. Ideally, a separate pool that is fed by water from the main pond will work best, but aquariums will also do the job. If you use an aquarium, be sure to use a sponge filter, so the fry do not get filtered out of the water with other small particles.

Young sanke may look dramatically different from the adult pictured here.

Feeding the fry can be quite demanding. If the container they are in does not have water from the main pond running through it, then you should replace about 20 percent of the container's water daily using water from the main pond. This will help to replace any of the microscopic infusoria that koi fry will need to supplement their diet. An alternative to feeding infusoria to your koi fry is to hatch out baby brine shrimp for them. This is a project in an of itself, and you will want to refer to a text that specifically deals with such topics as this process is beyond the scope of this book.

Feeding Baby Koi

When koi are small, 1 to 3 inches in total length (TL) for example, we feed them a growth food. This is usually a prepared food in the form of flakes or small pellets and is offered four to six times daily. This allows the juvenile koi to take in nutrients all day and keeps a steady flow of essential vitamins and minerals in the digestive system.

The use of small live foods or frozen foods is also highly encouraged while the fish are at this stage. During each feeding, you should feed the fish until their bellies are only slightly rounded off, not bulging and ready to burst. This is a perfect example of "quality, not quantity" because if you keep a strict regimen, they will not need a lot of food, use only good food and offer it to them several times a day. Since they are being fed so heavily, the water in their grow-out containers, or rearing ponds, must be changed frequently to ensure proper growth and development. Poor water quality also leads to disease and can have a lasting affect on the quality of the koi for long periods of time.

Adult female koi can produce more than 10,000 eggs during a single spawning, but fewer than a quarter of them are usually raised to adulthood. Culling the brood is vital. It is in this size range that you will be able to see which, if any, babies you will want to keep for yourself or as a potential source of income (to help offset the cost of this hobby) for the future.

Deformities are also apparent at this stage. While it is ultimately up to you as to what you do with them, most agree that it is better to cull the specimens that do not exhibit favorable traits. By doing this, you are further ensuring the success of those that do exhibit more desirable traits.

Foods high in alpha and beta-carotenes bring out the red in fishes.

Part 2

Feeding Juvenile Koi

Juvenile koi are considered the most common size in which koi are purchased for private koi ponds. Juveniles are usually considered

Children often love to feed koi, but just keep an eye on the amount they offer.

any fish over 3 inches TL and under 10 inches TL. This is a broad range of sizes but, surprisingly, they have very similar feeding guidelines.

As with the baby koi, these size classes need plenty of food, and the food must be of good quality in order to bring out the best qualities in the fish. It is generally agreed that fish in these size classes should be fed about three or four times daily. Feed them until their bellies are rounded and use as wide variety of foods.

Koi at this size will most definitely begin to become surface trained and surely can recognize their owners. These are traits that will only be strengthened with the use of good-quality foods. Your koi will know the difference, and they will prove it to you in the way they react to your offerings. A great reward treat to offer koi in this size range and larger is peas, whole or halved.

Feeding Adult Koi

Ironically, the feeding of adult koi does not mirror the feeding of baby and juvenile koi as one might expect. Koi go through several physiological changes as they grow and mature. One of these changes is the slowing down of their metabolism. Certainly all coldwater fish do this when the temperature falls below a certain level; however, adult koi do this as a sign of their maturity.

Koi measuring 12 inches or more are considered adults. When koi reach approximately 12 inches TL, they begin to expand in girth rather than length. It is at this stage that you will be able to distinguish between males and females with slightly more ease as compared to the smaller size classes. In general, females are broader due to their need to carry large quantities of eggs, so if you are shopping for adult koi and would like a trio (usually one male and two females), then 12 inches is the smallest size class you should begin looking at.

Adult koi do not have to be fed daily. If you live in an environment where the water temperature is in the low to mid-80s for the better part of the year, then the fish's metabolism may dictate more frequent feedings. You should, however, have sufficient shade and water depth to compensate for the increased water temperature. A general rule of thumb for feeding adult koi is the amount each fish

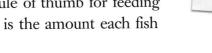
Patrick Grady is a professional koi keeper. Here he is offering food to a group of newly imported koi.

can consume in 30 to 40 seconds. The labels on most fish food packages instruct you to feed as much as your fish will consume in three to five minutes. Extremely large koi could eat almost the entire package of food in three to five minutes, so obviously that is not a good rule of thumb.

Because adult koi are so large, it is not easy to see when their bellies are "rounded off" as their bellies will always look that way if they are cared for properly so it is best to adjust your feedings using time. You will always have to fine-tune this technique as the amount of food these fish require will always be changing due to season, water temperature, amount of daylight, and breeding activity just to name a few. What you don't want is to throw in a large quantity of food only to return an hour or so later and see it uneaten in the water. This is a sure sign that you have over fed them and that can be very deadly.

Feeding Shamu

When the term, "adult," no longer adequately describes your koi because it has become enormously oversized, koi people often refer to that gigantic koi as being a "Shamu." Large Utsuri Mono or Bekko colored koi actually look like a small versions of the famous killer whale.

These koi do not necessarily need specialized diets, but they may require a larger-sized feed. If you feed a prepared feed, then you may need to buy a jumbo-sized pellet. Normal-sized pellets may go

Part 2

completely unnoticed by such large fish, and if left in the pond, they may cause the water quality to become depleted. Often, such huge koi are past their showing days and may even be past their reproductive days as well. If this is the case, and you are only feeding them to keep them alive, you may want to explore the use of a high-quality dog food for a staple diet, with regular offerings of peas and earthworms as treats every other or third day.

Large black-and-white koi actually look like small killer whales.

Dietary Supplements

The use of supplements in the diets of koi is largely unexplored. If you make your own prepared foods for your fish, then this will be an area that should be of considerable interest to you, as you can then add a wide assortment of ingredients to your homemade fish foods. If you rely on over-the-counter foods, such as those found at pet shops and pond-supply outlets, then the diets suggested above, in combination with those that work for your trusted suppliers, should work for you, too.

Here is a group of newly imported koi direct from Japan.

One of the best supplements to add to your koi's diet is bee pollen. Bee pollen will naturally help to increase and maximize coloration in koi and other fish as well. Bee pollen should be added raw to the food and exposed to as little heat as possible. This great and natural color additive is found at most natural food stores.

Another common and very effective food additive is *Spirulina* alga. The alga is sold as a powder and can be added to food formulations much like bee pollen can. *Spirulina* algae provide stabilized vitamins and minerals that are only found in marine algae. Colors will become enhanced with the use of this product, and it is a great source of natural plant matter.

Water Volume and Surface Area

The relationship between the water volume and the surface area of your pond is very important. Just because your pond is deep does not mean that it will be able to hold more fish than a shallow pond of a similar length and width. While the depth of a pond is important, shallow ponds are often capable of holding the

This indoor koi pond is large enough to house several large koi.

same amount of similarly sized fish, due to the surface to water volume ratio. This may seem confusing at first, but by the end of this chapter, you should fully understand this relationship and its significance in your pond keeping success.

To understand the relationship between water volume and surface area, let's use a 1200-gallon tank as an example. Not all ponds holding 1200 gallons are the same shape. Some may be wider than others or deeper than others, and many will have irregular shapes. Therefore, it should never be assumed that all ponds holding 1200 gallons are capable of holding the same number of fish.

A standard 150-gallon aquarium can be used as another example. This aquarium measures 72 inches long by 18 inches wide by 28 inches tall. This aquarium is capable of holding more fish of a similar size as compared with a 150-gallon show tank that measures 48 inches long by 24 inches wide by 30 inches tall. Why? Because the surface area to volume ratio is greater in the longer, shorter aquarium as compared to a taller, not-so-long aquarium.

Because the water has less contact time with the air in taller aquariums and in deeper ponds, the available oxygen is not replenished to its greatest extent. This can often lead to very poor oxygen levels (hypoxia) in the pond and may cause a large fish-kill. This is especially true in ponds that are exposed to high temperatures due to over-exposure to sunlight.

The Right-Sized Pond

When choosing a pond for your yard or garden, you should have a very well thought-out plan. A fairly significant portion of this plan deals with the eventual size of your pond when the construction is completed. That said; you might be in need of some helpful tips in arriving at the target-sized pond for your prized koi.

Building the right-sized pond initially will be very important in attaining your koi-keeping goals.

Part 2

The end result should encompass several things. The first and foremost is to allow enough space for a given number of koi to grow and thrive, not just to survive from day to day. Thriving fish means healthy, long-lived fish and a happy koi owner.

Second, the pond should be able to be serviced easily, because daily or bi-daily maintenance will be required to keep your koi in tip-top condition.

Third, the pond should be efficient, both in energy and nutrient consumption. You should have a high-quality filter and pump combination that will give you your best water movement and turnover rates. These systems are available from your local pond suppliers or aquarium shops and come in a vast assortment of sizes and flow rates. Your pond professional will consult you with this and see that you have the right equipment to get the job done and done right.

The Importance of Space

Koi are capable of growing to enormous sizes. As mentioned earlier, koi can grow to more than 40 inches in length and their close relative, the carp, is ranked as one of North America's largest game fishes. Certainly, their longevity has a role to play in this but so does space. Koi do not grow to these enormous sizes by living in small volumes of water, so a large pond is a must.

While the actual volume of water needed to grow koi to full size is highly controversial, it is safe to say that all the koi you own should have a minimum of 300 gallons per fish throughout their lives. That means that if you have a pond holding 1200 gallons of water, then you should house no more than four koi. This is true regardless of the size your koi are when you obtain them. To be on the safe side, a minimum of 400 gallons per fish is more respectable.

Koi, as well as other fishes, can have their growth stunted if they are not allowed enough swimming room. More often, they will suffer from chronic diseases, such as bacterial fin-rot, ICK, or velvet. These come about due to a suppressed immune system from overcrowding or cramped quarters and the poor water quality that is often associated with those living conditions. Therefore, space can have a significant influence on fish's health and vitality from day one, not just as large adults.

These numbers may be startling to you at first, especially if you are a beginner. However do not compare your pond to an aquarium as many hobbyists mistakenly do. There really is very little in common between them. The major reason for this is the relationship between water volume and surface area.

Stocking Density

The ratio of water volume to surface area is important in determining the proper number of fish you are able to safely and humanely house in a given volume of water. This is commonly referred to as the stocking density and is directly correlated to the amount of biomass a particular system (your pond) has in it. Biomass can be defined best as the amount of living matter within a system. Living matter includes all plants, animals, bacteria, and fungi. A system can be a lake, river, pond, aquarium, or may be a section of any of them as well.

The stocking density indicates how many fishes you can have in your pond.

Do not forget about other species of fishes in your pond. They are

Part 2

all considered biomass as well. Your plants, snails, insect larvae, small animals, turtle, frogs (and tadpoles), birds, and anything else that lives in and around your pond will have a direct influence on the overall biomass of your system. You must keep these things in mind when stocking your pond. Whether your pond is 100 gallons or 10,000 gallons, these factors are important to consider.

You may have a very difficult time looking at your brand new 1200-gallon pond and only seeing four koi swimming around in there as if they were guppies in a huge aquarium, but, theoretically, that is all that should be housed in there. However, theoretical numbers are simply numbers that would work best under a certain set of conditions or an environment. We all know that you can put more than four koi in a 1200-gallon pond, especially if they are small or intermediate-sized fish. But will they do as well as six or seven koi in that same 1200-gallon pond would? The answer may surprise you.

Koi ponds should be deep enough to allow the koi to avoid the winter and summer temperature extremes.

The truth is: yes and no. The answer is directly related to the amount of biomass in the pond, not the actual number of fish. So what does that mean? It means that if you have a 1200-gallon pond, then you can usually put more, smaller-sized koi in the pond or fewer, larger-sized koi in the same pond. The biggest problem you will then face is where that fine line is between overcrowding your pond and not overcrowding your pond.

To make your lives as easy as possible, always try to purchase koi around the same size. This will allow you to get a good handle on when it is time to sell some off as they grow down the road. Uniformity is always easier to deal with rather than fishes of various sizes. Also, bullies are more apt to develop with groups of different-sized fish, so there is another hidden benefit in doing this as well.

> Always keep in mind that even if you spend the money and buy some larger koi, chances are they are not full-grown. Even koi farmers are hard-pressed to find full-grown adults, so the chances of finding them at your local fish store or garden center are slim.

Part 2

It would not be fair to you, nor the fish, to give an opinion as to what sizes and numbers of specimens can be housed together. This is one of those areas that you will have to develop a feel for over a period of time. Certainly, your local pond dealer can assist you in this subject and advise you in the right direction. In time, you will find the right number of fish that seem to thrive for you in your setup, and it will all come together.

Part Three
Special Needs for Special Fish

"Did you ever just sit and wonder what makes them tick?"

Life Support for Your Koi

There are many ways to successfully maintain your koi pond. Some incorporate the use of high-tech equipment, while others require no equipment at all. Most ponds are best maintained by using a strategy that falls somewhere in between. Your pond dealer often acts as a consultant and will be able to assist you in choosing the right

Koi need good-quality filters in order to keep their pond water as clean as possible.

A well-balanced pond is an absolute necessity in order to keep your koi healthy.

equipment for your setup.

As previously mentioned, koi have the potential to become extremely large fish. Therefore, if your pond requires the use of a life support system, you will need one that is going to keep their water quality at its best. In most cases, dedicated koi owners have ponds that contain more than 2000 gallons of water, some having more than 10,000 gallons in volume. Therefore, these people must use one of the following options: several filters, one large filter, or several large filters in order to maintain the high-quality water these fish require.

Importance of the Nitrogen Cycle

In a nutshell, the nitrogen cycle is the process of converting a highly toxic nitrogen compound, in the form of ammonia, back to pure nitrogen. There are several steps involved here, and each one will be touched on specifically. For now, however, it is important to simply understand that such a process does take place and is the primary reason that one is not able to dump a large amount of fishes into your pond at one time. This is especially true with new ponds because the "spike" of ammonia will quickly cause the fish a lot of discomfort and can surely kill them should the ammonia levels become uncontrollably high.

For this reason, you should always take great care in breaking in or "cycling" your pond. To cycle your pond means to simply allow the bacterial species responsible for the breakdown of nitrogenous wastes enough time to develop and begin their duties. This time frame will vary depending on many conditions, such as the water temperature, volume of the pond, number of fish in the pond, amount of other biomass, pH and other water chemistry values of the pond water, and the presence of a suitable substratum for the beneficial bacteria to colonize.

The estimated time frame that is required to properly break in a pond is approximately three weeks. That number is simply an average and should in no way be taken as law. However, even if your pond cycles in a week, waiting a bit longer will do absolutely no harm whatsoever. Feel free to add a fish to the pond each week if you would like. There is no punishment for moving slowly while adding live animals to your pond. On the other hand, if you dump a bunch of fish in the pond, and the pond takes two weeks to calm down, then you must not think that you can make a habit out of continuing to dump in bunches of fish at one time. The biological backbone of the pond will break, and your pond will lose badly.

Part 3

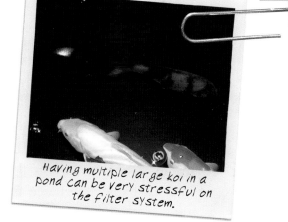

Having multiple large koi in a pond can be very stressful on the filter system.

The nitrogen cycle obviously plays a huge role in the success or failure of your pond experiences. That said, koi keepers certainly should get a better understanding as to the inter-workings of this cycle, so they will be able to identify the steps as they progress through the breaking-in process of their ponds.

Ammonia (NH3-)

The first step in the nitrogen cycle is, well, nitrogen. After all it is a cycle, not a one-way process. However, for all intents and purposes, ammonia is where we will start.

Ammonia is contained in the form of proteins in raw fish wastes and uneaten foodstuffs and is then excreted by the heterotrophic bacteria that consume these proteins. Proteins that are not used by the koi will be released as ammonia through the gills. In this form (usually free ammonia), it is extremely toxic and, as mentioned, can cause great suffering to your fish should the level get too high.

Ammonia is then broken down into a less toxic compound, called nitrite, by bacteria of the *Nitrosomonas* complex. This is completed by the separation of the hydrogen by the nitrogen and then binding the nitrogen with two oxygen atoms.

Ammonia removal is fairly easy. First, you can filter your water over freshly activated carbon that contains zeolite clay. Zeolite is an ionic-exchange substance that quickly converts harmful ammonia into a non-toxic substance. Be cautious when using any ionic-exchange substance and always make sure your water is free from any salts. This may pose a problem with ponds because people often salt their ponds to help prevent parasitic infestations of their fishes. However, salts will react or exchange ions with ionic-exchange resins more easily and then any converted ammonia will revert back to its free state. This

Healthy koi, such as these, will come over to you regardless of whether it's feeding time or not.

can sometimes lead to massive fish-kills in older ponds that are heavily stocked. Your best bet in preventing ammonia toxicity is to allow your pond to cycle for several weeks, allowing the beneficial bacteria to slowly take hold.

Nitrite (NO2)

Nitrite should be taken very seriously, for it, too, is a highly toxic substance. Though nitrite is not as harmful as ammonia in the same concentrations, it can still easily kill your koi and other fishes.

The nitrite compound is made up of one nitrogen atom and two oxygen atoms. In their lone states, neither element is toxic at a normal atmospheric pressure. However, when they are combined in the right amounts, they become a new substance, one that can kill your fish very quickly. Remember that polluted water may appear to be crystal clear but can still hold a high concentration of harmful substances. With this combination of oxygen and nitrogen, bacteria of the genus *Nitrobacter* are able to convert the nitrite into a less toxic nitrogen compound called nitrate. Nitrite is odorless so don't be fooled into believing that you can smell your water to see if it is bad.

The best defense against nitrite poisoning is to feed sparingly, remove any uneaten foodstuffs, perform regular water changes, and make all adjustments slowly as to prevent the beneficial bacteria bed from stressing out and dying off. If you find that your pond is showing a high nitrite reading, you can perform all of the same functions that you would do if your pond were suffering from a high ammonia concentration.

Nitrate (NO3)
Nitrate is the last breakdown and least harmful product in the nitrogen cycle. From here, any nitrate that is not converted back to free nitrogen and oxygen will be used to provide nutrients to any type of photosynthetic organism that you water comes in contact with. These include all species of plants and algae in your pond. As a matter of fact, old pondwater is often used to water your plants or garden, due to the high levels of nitrate, and other metabolites that are often found in it. Anaerobic bacteria will also consume nitrate, in which case nitrogen will be liberated and then the cycle will be completed.

Nitrate is not usually found in high concentration in natural bodies of water. Therefore, many fish, even koi, will only tolerate so much. Keeping the overall nitrate level below 50 mg/L is best, as anything higher than that may cause acute toxicity over long periods of time. Remember to perform partial water changes and not to overfeed.

Maintaining Good Water Quality

Koi are rather tough fish that do well in a broad range of water chemistry. However, even hardy fishes can succumb to poor water quality. This is especially true if the water quality remains poor over long periods of time. Water quality can encompass several things.

First, it can directly refer to a certain property of water. For example, the quality of a pond's water can be con-sidered poor due to the lack of dissolved minerals. This water would not have a high general hardness, so the water may be considered poor.

Second, water quality may be con-sidered poor due to the temperature. Water temperature is a huge factor in determining overall water quality, as water at higher temperature is often more apt to have stabilization problems regarding bacteria count and algae blooms. Therefore, water temperature is often looked at when determining overall water quality.

One of the most important life support features for a large koi pond is an air blower.

Water gardens, such as this one, show just how beautiful a well-balanced koi pond can be.

More commonly, however, water quality refers to the amount of dissolved metabolites that are contained in the water. Metabolites can most simply be thought of as products of metabolic processes. For example, when fish breath, they release carbon dioxide and, in that case, carbon dioxide is a metabolite. Fish also excrete nitrogenous wastes in the form of ammonia and urea. Both of these are products of digestion and are considered metabolites as well. Because metabolites are always being produced, they must be controlled in such a way as to prevent them from building up to the point where they have a negative affect on your water quality.

The most effective way to remove metabolites in pondwater is to perform partial water changes on a regular basis, meaning once every two or three weeks for desirable results. Water changes should become an integral part of your maintenance routine with your pond. Some of the signs that your fish may be suffering from metabolite toxicity are: labored breathing at the water's surface, head and lateral line degeneration, chronic disease outbreaks (especially bacterial infections), listlessness or lazy behavior, and feeding irregularity. Most of the time, when conditions are corrected and brought back to more favorable parameters, the signs and symptoms rapidly reverse. Again, always try to perform regular, partial water changes and do not overfeed your koi.

Filtration For Your Koi Pond

There are three types of common filtration for all ponds or aquariums: biological, mechanical, and chemical filtration. They are equally important to each other but are often misun-derstood. Many of the pond filters that are available from your local garden center or pond dealer provide all three of these types, or steps, of filtration. However, you should have a thorough understanding of each step and what roles they play in keeping your koi happy and healthy.

The size of your pond and the volume of water that it holds direct-ly influence the type of filtration device you should use in order to

provide the best, most efficient filtration possible. Many people also prefer to custom build their own filters. Most of the time, this is perfectly accept-able, but there are significant engineering methods that need to be utilized. Unfortu-nately, even though some people have good intentions and may even be trying to save some cash, it is often not worth the effort.

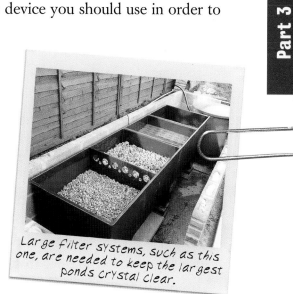

Large filter systems, such as this one, are needed to keep the largest ponds crystal clear.

Biological Filtration

Biological filtration is the breakdown of organic and non-organic compounds into less toxic and/or simpler substances. The nitrogen cycle that was mentioned at the beginning of this chapter is only one of several cycles that actually take place within an ecosystem–yes, your pond is an ecosystem. Carbon is perhaps the next-most important cycle that is looked at in environmental sciences. The carbon cycle is basically the flow of carbon within the ecosystem, particularly in the food web. Carbon is another substance that can sometimes be considered a metabolite but, more commonly, carbon must be chemically adhered to another element to form a molecule, such as in carbon dioxide, mentioned previously.

Efficient biological filtration is best achieved by having raw pondwater flowing over a medium that is suitable for the colonization of beneficial bacteria species, such as those that are responsible for the breakdown of nitrogenous compounds. Some examples of good-quality mediums for positive recruitment of these beneficial bacteria include: course foam, lava rock, tufa rock, coral rock (in low pH situations), plastic bio-balls, plastic pipe pieces, Japanese filter matting, filter brushes, flint gravel, and porcelain pieces. All of these materials and more are widely available at many common retail outlets that provide pond filtration units.

The velocity of the water flowing over your biological filter should be moderate, not so rapid that no buildup can take place. Conversely, the water flow shouldn't be too slow either, as this will encourage sediment to settle and prevent the materials from becoming colonized with beneficial bacteria. Many ready-made filter/pump kits solved this problem by providing the correctly sized water pump along with the filtration unit that you are purchasing.

This photo shows a good example of how large some filter systems are.

Figuring out the flow rate that is required to properly filter your pond can be tricky and demanding. That is one more reason to not only purchase a pump/filter kit, but it is also reason to seek the advice of professionals that work with filters and pumps on a regular basis. They will be able to help you answer questions that will certainly arise, especially if they involve custom setups.

Part 3

Mechanical Filtration

Mechanical filtration is simply the physical process of removing suspended debris from the water column. Good-quality mechanical filters will provide your pond's water with a polished look that appears to be reflective in nature. Often, mechanical filtration materials are the first materials that the raw water from the pond comes in contact with. This helps to reduce the possibility of soil deposition on the biological filter material as well as within the chemical filtering media.

Bunched plants not only provide oxygen but also provide a medium where suspended particles can be filtered out of the water.

Materials that are suitable for mechanical filtration usage are: angel hair, fine foam rubber, filter felt, poly fiber, cotton (no longer common), micron cartridges (many canister filters use these), and sand. All of these materials are commonly available through your local pond dealer or garden center and are often in the form of replaceable cartridges that are easily disposed of when soiled. Only one, sand, is difficult and messy to use.

Sand is often used in pressurized canister filter setups that were originally designed for swimming pools. Sand can be packed very tightly, allowing almost zero penetration of suspended particulate matter. It takes a tremendous amount of pressure and force to pull the water through the sand, and clogs are almost certain unless the system is back-flushed every few days. Back-flushing is the process in which a filter's flow is reversed and the soiled water is redirected out into another area, such as a garden, septic tank, or sewer. Needless to say, sand is not commonly used due to its high maintenance and tendency to clog.

Another type of mechanical filtration is known as foam fractionation. This is the process of attaching air molecules to hydrophobic (water-hating) materials. These materials are often inorganic in nature and are not capable of dissolving in water or any other liquid environment. Foam fractionators are tall, cylindrical pieces of equipment that afford the longest possible contact time between water and tiny air bubbles that are injected into the system via a venturi air valve. Venturi air valves draw in a certain amount of air based on the water that is flowing through them. The more water flow you have, the more air you get injected into the reaction chamber. The reaction chamber is where the air bubbles attach themselves to the hydrophobic particles. Once air has attached to particles, the particles begin to rise, while the "clean" water is denser and flows out of the system into the pond. The particles will be collected in a collection cup located at the top of the reaction chamber. The product is usually very clean and crystal-clear pond water.

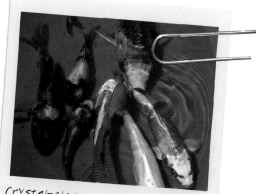

Crystal-clear water like this is the result of high-quality filtration.

Part 3

Chemical Filtration

Chemical filtration is a method that incorporates three basic types: chemicals that neutralize or detoxify harmful chemicals; absorption materials, such as activated carbon; and ionic-exchange resins, such as zeolite clay. All three have their own uses in the koi pond but perhaps none is as popular as the use of activated carbon.

Activated carbon is available in many different grades. Many of the different grades are very close in absorptive value as the next. The only grade that is universally considered worthless is the "raw" grade. This grade has almost no pores on the surface of each bit, and therefore does not have a very high surface area, translating into a low absorptive value. The higher grades of carbon are very porous and thus have a high absorptive value. This high absorptive value usually works to your advantage, though sometimes it can actually work against it. High-grade activated carbon will absorb toxins and contaminants so quickly that the carbon becomes "spent" and will need to be replaced more often than lesser grades.

There are assorted types of chemical additives that may or may not be helpful in a koi pond. Many of these will neutralize heavy metals or toxins such as chlorine and/or chloramines. They have a limited use, however, due to the fact that they usually produce either precipitates or other by-products that, in turn, will cause acute toxicity if allowed to build up. There are also several chemical additives that can be associated with biological filtration because they contain products that stimulate the beneficial bacteria populations that are required for a well-balanced pond. That, however, may be a stretch in terms of lumping them into the "chemical filtration" group.

Chemicals can be tricky to use. Always ask for assistance if you have any questions whatsoever, as overdosing even the weakest solution can lead to death of your fish

Miscellaneous Equipment

There are literally dozens of extra pieces of equipment and assorted other products that you will accumulate throughout your koi-keeping career (sometimes spanning a lifetime). These will include: just about every type and size of koi foods that are, or have been, available; various filters and pumps; feeding rings; tubing

Pond netting is a useful piece of equipment used to prevent critters from getting at your prized koi.

of all sizes and lengths; PVC hard piping; the glue and primer to go with the hard piping; various holding containers, from old bath tubs to ten-gallon aquariums and everything in between; and lastly, nets and other capturing devices.

Nets and Koi Socks

Most of the normally sized aquarium nets will suffice for capturing koi for their first year of life. After that, they are just about worthless unless you keep them around for skimming the dead insects and leaves off of the pond's surface. Once they reach a year old, many koi are just too beefy and far too fast to be caught in these conventional-sized nets. Even the types marketed as "long-handled" nets are way too short to reach koi in even the most common-sized ponds.

You should gently guide the captured koi out of the capture device.

Nets for capturing koi should be soft to the touch. Even though koi have rather tough scales, they can be sloughed off fairly easily, leaving the fish open to infection. They should also have long handles, meaning at least 4 feet in total length. There are also many nets that have the ability to be expanded. These usually go in one-half-foot increments and may be as long as 8 feet. There are longer ones, but you will trade in rigidity for length with these nets. Sometimes, especially with big koi, you need all the rigidity you can get. Remember that these fish can weigh over ten pounds as young adults.

There is another capture device that is worth mentioning here: the koi sock. Essentially, the koi sock is an open-ended net made from a very soft and flexible material that feels like silk– sometimes, expensive ones *are* made of silk. They are thin and elongated, sometimes more than 4 feet long, and are meant for capturing only one fish at a time. The idea behind them is for the fish to swim into the end that you are holding (the one with the handle) and then you reach down and pinch off the other end with your other hand. This leaves the fish situated in one direction and unable to turn around. When you pick the fish up, the water slowly drains from all around the fish, leaving them in a soft, wet material where they are hard-pressed to do damage to their fins and scales. The fish can then be placed in whatever container they are going in with little concern as to having to untangle them from a net or getting their fins stuck in nets and so on.

Holding & Examination Containers

When you purchase a new koi from a retailer or any other source, you should always examine the specimen that you plan on adding to your collection. In order to do this with as little stress as possible, always place the fish in a holding container or an examination container. Essentially, they are one and the same; however, holding containers are usually designed for housing the fish for a longer

Plastic laundry baskets make great holding containers for koi of all sizes.

Part 3

period of time than a regular examination would take.

Examination containers are usually shallow containers that force the fish to list to one side or another. This allows the potential buyer or inspector to see the sides, or flanks, of the specimen being examined. Normally, the fish only spends no longer than ten minutes in one of these containers and often less than five minutes. Some good ideas for homemade examination containers are plastic shoeboxes and shallow tote boxes.

The container should be drilled as to allow some water drainage or flow through it. You can drill holes in the container by using a good-quality drill bit of any normal size. First you situate the box to be drilled in such a way as to prevent the container from slipping– the last thing you want to do is drill your finger. Next, place the drill on high speed and situate the drill bit in the area you want your first hole to be punched. Now activate the drill but *do not* place a lot of pressure on the plastic. The drill bit will begin to heat up due to friction, and it will assist you in making the hole by melting the plastic as you push it through.

Once all of your holes have been drilled you must feel each one to make sure they are smooth. Usually they will be if you have taken your time, as the drill bits will remain quite warm throughout the process and will leave a small amount of melted plastic bordering each edge of the holes. If there are any holes that remain rough, you can use a nail file to smooth them over.

Small koi are easily observed in a holding container, such as this one.

Holding containers serve a similar purpose as examination containers. However they are better suited to hold the koi for longer periods of time. Usually they are placed in holding containers within the main pond itself–assuming a quarantine period has been completed. Holding containers allow the fish to become acclimatized to their new surroundings and the water chemistry of the main pond. They also allow the hobbyist to make sure that the fish is feeding and behaving normally. New koi can be harassed by the original residents of the pond, so holding containers also allow the older koi acclimatize to the newer ones.

Automatic Feeders & Feeding Rings

Feeding your koi should be enjoyable for the whole family. Sometimes the family will not be available to feed your fish, so you must rely on another source. This source is most commonly a device known as an automatic fish feeder. Automatic fish feeders come in a variety of styles and sizes and can often be adjusted as to how much food they can offer your fish.

Automatic fish feeders can also be used to supplement your feedings because they are often adjustable. For example, if you feed your koi small meals several times each day, and you are unable to be at home during midday, then an automatic feeder is probably the best way to deliver those feedings at the times your fish are accustomed to getting them. Continued feeding schedules may mean the difference between life and death over winter months in particular. Also, automatic fish feeders are a good choice for weekend trips.

The intense red coloration on this sanke is a result of regular feedings of good foods.

These devices do, however, have their fair share of flaws. The most commonly encountered flaw in many designs of automatic feeders is the moisture buildup. Moisture will cause the food to grow fungus and spoil within hours of exposure. An easy way of

Part 3

preventing this would be to make some holes in the container that holds the food, but then you run the risk of spoiling the fish food due to exposure to open air. Therefore, the easiest way to prevent moisture buildup in the container is to mount the feeder away from any water devices that splash water, such as waterfalls, fountainheads, and pump returns.

Another commonly encountered flaw that some koi hobbyists experience with automatic feeders is the failure of the unit to feed your fish. This may occur for several reasons. The first is the batteries, so always make sure that the batteries in the feeder are fresh. Most feeders have a "test" button that allows you to simply test the batteries should you believe that the feeder is not delivering the food as it was programmed. The next issue is the food not falling out of the feeder. This can occur due to improper size of food (usually too large for the holes in the feeder) or may occur because the feeding regulator has malfunctioned. Always be sure to read the manufacturer's instruction booklet that accompanies your feeder. This booklet can be long, but it will certainly give you troubleshooting advice for the future, and it is well worth the time it takes to look it over.

Feeding rings can be a koi owner's best friend. As many of you know, koi can be difficult to surface train. This is especially true if the koi were raised in earth ponds where they did not receive daily attention. When they make their way into man-made ponds, they are usually quite timid. Feeding rings will assist you in breaking them in and letting them know that you are there to feed them, not to feed on them.

By using a feeding ring, you concentrate the food offered within the confines of the ring. This produces competition and causes fish to race toward the ring and the food within it. New fish quickly get the hang of this and begin feeding at a quicker pace. After the desired results are achieved, you can remove the feeding ring until another new addition is added to the collection.

Part Four
Under the Weather

"Not feeling well? Are you getting enough liquids?
Oh, wait, silly question."

Common Diseases and Their Treatments

Koi, like all fish, will occasionally contract diseases. Some are more serious than others; however, the majority can be treated with common drugs available from your veterinarian or local aquarium store. The most common diseases that affect koi are external diseases. External diseases can include several species of bacteria,

Butterfly koi are highly susceptible to bacterial fin and tail rot.

parasites, protozoan parasites, and fungi. Of these, the most common are protozoan parasitic infections.

Parasitic Protozoan Outbreaks

Most protozoa are free-living, meaning they do not attach themselves to a host. There are some that do, however, attach themselves to a host. In this case, we are concerned with those that attach themselves to fishes. Several species of parasitic protozoa are quite common but are easily detected and treated successfully if caught before they have any chance of over-running their host.

Costia (*Ichthyobodo necator*)

The smallest parasite that affects koi is known as costia, *Ichthyobodo necator*. Costia can live in water ranging from 35°F to 85°F but is most common when temperatures are in the lower portion of that range. Costia infections can be severe and lead to death if not treated. Because the parasite is so small, it is not easily noticed in its initial stages–only when skin lesions begin to appear will it have a chance to be correctly identified. Koi that are affected by this pathogen are at a high risk of contracting secondary infections, due to these open lesions. One of the most common secondary infections that occur are fungal infections, so be sure to watch for any cotton-like growths on any lesions that may be afflicting your koi caused by a costia infection.

Chilodonella piscicola

Another cool-water protozoan that commonly affects koi is

Part 4

Chilodonella piscicola, or simply chilodonella. This parasite will also do well in water with a high salt level (brackish). For this reason, *C. piscicola* does not respond well to salt treatments that would normally be effective in treating outbreaks of other parasites. Similar to costia, *C. piscicola* punctures the fish's skin cells and may result in skin lesions. Secondary infections are common and may result in fungal or bacterial infections.

ICK (*Ichthyophthirius multifiliis*)

The most common and recognizable species of parasitic protozoan is white spot disease, *Ichthyophthirius multifiliis*, or simply ICK for short. These parasites cause the infected fish to break out in white spots that are most noticeable on the clear parts of the fish's fins. If the disease remains untreated, the parasite will begin to pop up all over the fish's body and may even infect the gills. If the gills are infected, the fish may die from permanent damage that results from the protozoan feeding on the cells of the gills.

When you see these white spots appear, you should immediately take action by adding a remedy to the water, or more preferably, remove the infected fish from the main pond and treat in a separate hospital aquarium. As with most parasitic infections, usually multiple fish will be affected at one time, so medication of the pond itself may be necessary.

Trichondina spp.

Perhaps the most easily recognized protozoa are those of the

Trichodina complex. Trichodina is not a parasite that readily feeds on the fish's skin cells. Instead, it feeds on the bacteria and organic detritus that have become trapped within the mucus layer covering the fish. Heavy infestation indicates an environmental problem, and treatment calls for frequent, medium-scale water changes and gravel vacuuming. You may also wish to clean your filter piping with pipe brushes and any other locations that may trap organic detritus, as this protozoan does not even need to be in the presence of a fish in order to survive.

Flukes

In general, flukes are usually found in water with a high degree of organic detritus, low oxygen levels, and a high stocking density. By keeping your fish's environment clean and well aerated, you will help reduce infestations of these and other potentially harmful parasites.

Koi that spend a lot of time at the water's surface may have gill flukes.

Skin Flukes (*Gyrodactylus* sp.)

There are two basic categories of flukes that are associated with fishes: skin flukes and gill flukes. Skin flukes differ from gill flukes in that they do not have eyes and give birth to live young. Severe infestations of these parasites are often referred to as "gray slime disease" or, more commonly, they are misidentified as a protozoan parasitic infestation.

Gill Flukes (*Dactylogyrus* sp.)

Gill flukes are distinguished by four small, black eyespots on the head end of the body. They attach themselves to the gills of the fish and release their eggs by taking advantage of the pumping action of the fish's breathing. The water temperature is directly responsible for the speed of the eggs' hatching. Heavy infestations of gill flukes will often cause the tips of the gills' membranes to grow in odd shapes and thus decreases their efficiency.

Anchor Worms & Fish Lice

The most clearly visible parasites that you may encounter are anchor worms and fish lice. These parasites can cause serious injury to your koi, and these injuries may lead to life-threatening, secondary bacterial infections. There are several liquid remedies available to combat these super-parasites. Your local aquarium and pond-supply store will be able to give you the one that works best for them.

Anchor worms (*Lernaea cyprinacea*)

Anchor worms have a rather complicated life cycle. The female is the only one that is parasitic, and her thread-like body usually sports a pair of white-colored eggs. These eggs are released into the water, where they will hatch, and the lifecycles of the young begin. The rate at which they grow is entirely dependent on the water

Part 4

Remove any anchor worms and treat the area with an antiseptic.

temperature and amount of food available. Once sexual maturity is reached, the males and females congregate on the gills of the fish to be infected. After mating, the males die and the females crawl along the fish to find a suitable site to implant their "anchors." During the time the females are attached, they will feed heavily on blood and tissue from the fish in order to nourish their developing eggs. The process is then repeated by the next generation of young.

Fish lice (*Argulus japonicus*)

Fish lice can also be pests to your koi. They are most commonly found around the gills but, in extreme infestations, they can literally be crawling over the whole body of the infected fish. Fish lice will feed on koi during all stages of their growth and development. They do this by puncturing the skin with their needle-like feeding appendages to suck blood and other bodily juices from the fish. By doing this, fish lice can easily transmit bacterial and viral diseases to the host fish. Fish lice are very active swimmers, and the females lay their eggs among blanketweed, duckweed, or other floating plants where they will usually hatch in four to six weeks, depending on environmental temperatures.

Treating Parasitic Diseases

Treating koi for parasitic ailments is usually quite successful, but you should always take great care when using any medication so as not to overdose. It is important to know the full volume of your pond and be sure to include the volume of the filter system and any piping and other equipment that may hold a significant volume of water. Always have someone check your dosing because it is very easy to make a simple mistake when you are dealing with decimal points. What follows is a list of common and effective medications that will assist you in treating the majority of parasitic diseases that you will encounter.

Acriflavine

Uses: Treats external parasitic, bacterial, and fungal infections
Dose: 6-12 mg/L dissolved in water
Acriflavine is a rather weak medication that is most commonly used to treat external parasites, such as ICK and Costia, when they are in their early stages of development. Acriflavine will stain the water a bright yellow/green color and may permanently stain clothes a dark brown color should you get some on them. Over the years, the effectiveness of acriflavine has decreased, due to an immunity that many parasite species have built against it. For this reason, you may wish to explore some of the more contemporary and stronger medications on the market.

Formalin

Uses: Treats external parasitic infestations

Part 4

Dose: 40 percent solution at 15-25 mg/L
Formalin is one of the most effective anti-parasitic treatments on the market. It is used for just about any external ailment in varying dosages and concentrations. For more detailed information regarding the proper use of this drug, you should consult a veterinarian. Formalin is a gill irritant and may decrease the level of dissolved oxygen in the water, so be sure to follow recommended directions very carefully.

Leteux Meyer Mixture
Uses: Treats external parasitic infestations
Dose: 0.1 mg malachite green mixed with 25 mg/L Formalin
Leteux Meyer solution is a mixture of malachite green and Formalin. This combination proves very effective against the more stubborn external parasitic infestations. Several companies produce this as a ready-made mixture, and you should use one of those rather than attempt to mix your own.

Malachite Green
Uses: Treats external parasitic infestations and fungal infections
Dose: 0.1 mg/L. There are also malachite green solutions available, and those should be used as directed by the manufacturer.
Malachite green is an effective solution to many common external parasitic and fungal infections. However, the use of this medication is controversial, as it is thought to contain cancer-causing agents. For that reason, you should never allow yourself to come in direct contact with the solution or water treated with the medication.

Always use supplementary aeration when treating with malachite green because it is know to reduce the oxygen level of the water.

Potassium Permanganate

Uses: Treats protozoan parasitic and bacterial infections on the skin and gills

Dose: 2 mg/L (in powder form)

Potassium permanganate is a very effective environmental-cleansing solution that destroys organic molecules and helps clarify pondwater. You should check your pH prior to using this chemical. The higher the pH, the more toxic it will be to your fish and other pondlife. You may have to repeat the dosage frequently with this medication because the higher the percentage of organic material in the system, the more of the chemical it takes to achieve the desired results. You should not use this chemical in the presence of salt or Formalin.

Common salt (sodium chloride)

Uses: Treats common parasitic and fungal infections

Dose: 3 gm/L for prolonged immersion

Salt is the oldest know treatment for external protozoan infestations. Various authorities have published dosages that sometimes differ greatly in their effectiveness. Studies indicate that the presence of a low amount of salt in your pondwater will effectively prevent minor breakouts of common parasites. Keep in mind that salt will not breakdown, so only partial water changes will remove it from your system.

Part 4

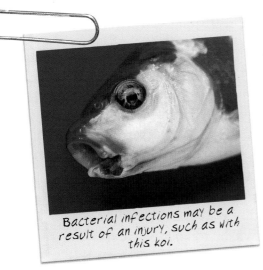

Bacterial infections may be a result of an injury, such as with this koi.

Bacterial Infections

Many species of bacteria, including those potentially harmful species, occur in every body of water containing fishes. It is much easier on both you and the fish if you take preventative measures from day one rather than rely on treatment measures down the road. Even in the best system, there will still be occasional outbreaks of disease, so it is important to be informed about how to minimize your fish's chances of contracting these pathogens. Koi will often respond well to common drugs available through your local dealer; however, there will be times where more powerful medications or a veterinarian who specializes in fishes will be needed.

Perhaps the most commonly encountered species of dangerous bacteria is *Aeromonas hydrophilia*, an opportunist that takes advantage of injured, sick, or weakened koi. Symptoms of an *Aeromonas* infection usually result in open lesions and severe ulceration of the fish's body. Over the years, this pathogen has become increasingly resistant to common antibiotics and is cause for some concern.

Ulceration is the most common problem associated with *Aeromonas* infections. Ulcers develop by the bacteria first gathering in large numbers on the skin surface. If left unchecked, these areas will develop a reddish coloration (which is the bacteria eating the skin) and soon thereafter, a small hole will begin to appear in the skin. Once the bacteria break through the outer protection of the fish (skin, scales, mucus coat), they will enter the bloodstream and may cause other problems, such as popeye and dropsy. If left untreated, your fish will certainly succumb to this bacterial infection.

Fungal Infections

If your koi become overly stressed for long periods of time, a fungal infection may present itself. More often than not, any infection will be bacterial. However, if the fungal spore count in the water is higher than the bacterial spore count, then a fungal infection is inevitable.

Fungal infections occur due to the breakdown of the integrity of the fish's skin. Once the fish is infected, the fungus appears as a cotton-like web growing over the fish's body. The fungus also takes on a gray or brown color because it traps any floating detritus in the pondwater and takes on its color. In ponds where the water is green from free-swimming algae, the infected fish will appear green, signaling a serious problem. Fungal infections spread very quickly, so if you notice that your koi are infected by it, remove the infected fish and treat them at once.

Part 4

Viral Infections

Viral infections are not curable. However, it is very rare for well-kept

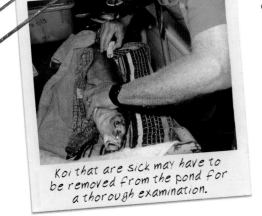

Koi that are sick may have to be removed from the pond for a thorough examination.

captive fishes to suffer from a virus. The only way you will normally get a viral infection is if your koi are subjected to wild carp from rivers or streams. The most common virus that koi may suffer from is known as carp pox. This virus is very similar to the one that causes herpes in humans. Carp pox is visible on the body and fins as white lumpy masses that will usually go away once the water temperatures increase in spring and summer.

Occasionally the lumps will remain with the fish for several years, only to disappear mysteriously one day.

Treating Bacterial and Fungal Diseases

The treatment of bacterial and fungal diseases can be difficult and frustrating. Often, they are far advanced, and your fish may already be showing signs of severe distress. Therefore, immediate action is needed. The most important thing that you can do is to remove your diseased specimen into a quarantine aquarium or pond. Quarantine aquariums and ponds allow you to not only observe the situation but to also effectively treat the specimen. The treatment of sick fishes should be carried out in a quarantine aquarium or other isolation container all the time. You never know when you may have a new strain of pathogen that happens to be immune to common drugs, so it's always better to play it safe.

Part 4

There are many types of antibiotics and antifungal medications that you have to choose from. Do not, however, feel that you can simply pick one that you think will suit your fish's needs. It is important to not only properly identify what is causing your fish discomfort but also to understand what is needed to treat it quickly and safely.

Often, there are several forms of one antibiotic. Examples are sulfa-based drugs. Some of these contain only one or two sulfa-based antibiotic/antifungal active ingredients, while others contain as many as five active ingredients. Again, it is extremely important to fully understand what is wrong with your fish *before* you begin medicating them. If you do not know, ask someone who does. The following is a list of general antibiotics/antifungal medications that are commonly available. Several of these antifungal drugs also work as antiparasitic medications, so please refer to the previous list of medications designed to treat them.

Ampicillin
Dose: Usually in capsule form. One capsule to ten gallons
Uses: A broad-range antibiotic
Ampicillin is effective against a wide range of gram-negative and gram-positive bacteria. It is most effective at treating the various bacteria that cause popeye (exophthalmia).

Furazolidone
Dose: Usually in capsule form. One capsule to ten gallons
Uses: Broad-range antimicrobial agent

Furazolidone is a nitrofuran-based antibiotic/antimicrobial agent that is potent and very effective in treating external diseases caused by high organic detritus that may result in the deterioration of environment.

Griseofulvin
Dose: Prescription only. Consult your local veterinarian.
Uses: Antifungal agent
Griseofulvin is a very powerful and effective antifungal medication that is currently available only through your local veterinarians. It treats a broad range of common fungal species that, if left untreated, would cause permanent disfigurement or death to your koi.

Metronidazole
Dose: Usually in capsule form but may be in tablet form. One capsule/tablet (250 mg) to ten gallons
Uses: Antibacterial/antiprotozoal agent
Metronidazole is a very effective drug that is used to prevent and cure common protozoal diseases. However, it is more commonly used as an antibiotic, so it is listed here. Metronidazole is available in one form or another in many pet shops and pond centers where aquatic medications are sold. Be sure to follow all manufacturers' directions carefully.

Oxytetracycline
Dose: Usually available in capsule form. One capsule to ten gallons
Uses: Coldwater specific, broad-range antibiotic
Oxytetracycline is commonly used in the aquaculture industry to

treat trout and salmon for bacterial infections. The use of this product in its common form may cause an orange discoloration of your water. This drug is most effective against gram-negative bacteria and should only be used if its proper identification can be verified.

Sulfa-based medications

Dose: Usually available in both capsule and tablet form. One capsule to ten gallons, dosage varies with tablet form.

Uses: Antibacterial/Antifungal

There are many types of sulfa-based drugs available to the average hobbyist. You should only use one of these treatments if you are able to correctly identify what you are treating. Fungal diseases often have similar symptoms to that of parasitic protozoan diseases, so be careful when deciding on treatment.

Tetracycline

Dose: Usually in capsule form. One capsule to ten gallons

Uses: Broad-range antibiotic

This is perhaps the most commonly used drug aside from standard penicillin. Many of today's strains of bacteria show some degree of immunity against tetracycline, probably due to its general use with anything that is considered "sick." Regarding ponds and its effectiveness in treating koi for common bacterial infections, you will have mixed results.

Dips and Baths

There are times when a fish is so diseased that it is not feasible, nor

Part 4

Several koi can be quarantined together.

advisable, to treat the fish in the main pond. In these situations, you will need to set up a dip or bath in order to effectively treat the infected fish. Times like this are frustrating because the fish are often in large enclosures and catching them requires a lot of skill and hard work. Chasing koi around these types of enclosures can also add to the stress and lead to further health problems.

Treating your koi with a dip is similar to a "flea dip" that you would give your cat or dog. Dips are most effective against parasitic infestations because the parasites are usually external and the medication in the dip solution comes in direct contact to the pathogen. Bacteria and fungi need to be immersed in the solution for longer periods of time, so a bath is a better option for their treatment.

External parasites can be treated with a variety of medications using the dipping technique. The most common, and most effective some argue, is common salt (sodium chloride). Salt is the oldest known treatment of parasites for captive fishes. The most effective formula for giving a sick koi a "salt bath" is 20 gm salt per liter for ten minutes. The water should have a stabilized pH and be heavily aerated. Other medications that can be used effectively for treating external parasitic infections on koi include: acriflavine, malachite green, and dylox (use extreme caution).

Baths are perfect options for chronic or reoccurring bacterial and fungal infections. One of the best-known baths used to treat fungi on fishes is a bath using warm water (75°F) and one drop of liquid methylene blue to one quart of water. Smaller koi and other pondfish will not take this very well, but larger koi will do okay. Always be sure that the fish have adjusted to the water temperature of the bath water prior to adding the medication. Using a bathing solution of this strength will almost always cause the mucus coating of the fish to become stained. This is okay and actually acts as a bandage, while also exposing the fungus to the intensity of the medication.

Baths do not do so well for bacterial infections overall. Some people have had good results using various herbal elements, such as tea tree oil, aloe, and even eucalyptus oil. These holistic medications have their place in koi keeping, but you should always have access to some of the proven-to-work medications that are on the market.

Medicated Feeds

Another method that is used to deliver doses of medication to targeted fish is medicated feeds. Usually in pelletized form, these feeds are very effective in delivering regular doses of key medications to infected koi. Medicated feeds are normally impregnated with Oxytetracycline because aquaculturists raising trout or salmon as food fish most commonly incorporate this

Part 4

The Medicine Cabinet

If you are serious about keeping koi and keeping them healthy, then you should have access to the following drugs and supplies on demand.

Common aquarium salt	Latex or vinyl gloves
Methylene blue solution	Holding container for the largest fish in your collection
Potassium permanganate	
Accurate measuring cup	Cotton swabs
Tweezers	Iodine or other topical antimicrobial solution

You should never keep a stockpile of antibiotics for a few reasons. First, they do not have long expiration dates, so you should only buy them when you need them; this way, they are as fresh as possible and are thus, more effective. Second, if they are housed at an improper temperature they may go bad and become ineffective. Lastly, children may find them and ingest them.

method. Koi, just like trout and salmon, are a coldwater species, and Oxytetracycline is a coldwater specific drug.

Medicated feeds are available through special order by most local pond retailers or through aquaculture-supply outlets. Their use varies and is most often based on the weight of the infected fish. You may need to consult your local veterinarian for proper feeding instructions.

Preventative Measures

The prevention of many common diseases in koi is possible through a healthy diet that is varied and nutritious, keeping their environment clean and free of excess wastes, and by not overstocking their ponds. Koi that are subjected to cramped conditions usually do not live long. One of the best ways to tell if your pond is overstocked is doing regular water tests for nitrates. If your nitrate level is sky-high even though you do regular, partial water changes, then you may have an overstocking problem to deal with. Another indicator of overstocked conditions is if your fish are always afflicted by some disease or disorder. For example, chronic parasitic infections are a telltale sign that something isn't right. Use what you have gained from this book and others to compare the current living conditions of your koi with those of known success stories.

Part Five

Seasons
of the Koi

Seasons of the Koi

Koi Reproduction

Koi are bred very successfully in the Far East, Israel, Europe, United States, and South Africa. However, Japan is still considered the epicenter of quality koi production. The breeding of high-grade koi is not only a science, but it's an art. In Japan, it is not uncommon for a koi breeder to spend a lifetime developing and ultimately

Koi reproduce by the thousands. Here is a group of the previous year's grow-outs.

This large, female platinum ogon is ripe with eggs.

perfecting a single strain of koi. Often, the task of doing this cannot be completed in one lifetime and thus, the development of the desired strain is passed along to the next generation. The professional breeders of Japan are not in any rush to produce the best koi in the world. In many people's opinions, they already do.

To purposely breed your koi for desirable traits is often a demanding process. It is demanding on you as the keeper and the fish as well. Large male koi can be relentless on the gravid females that are housed in the same pond as them. Ironically, if they are left alone, they will readily spawn by themselves. No attention will be paid to their looks by the koi though, of course.

Spawning usually takes place in late spring to early summer. Occasionally, they will spawn again in early autumn. When this happens, they call it the second spawn.

The purposeful spawning of koi in order to achieve desired color varieties and strains is far beyond the scope of this book. Therefore, we will focus on what you will need to ensure that your broodstock (the adult koi used for breeding) is conditioned properly and has suitable spawning sites, and that you are educated on the care of the young koi should you be fortunate enough to get some. It is strongly recommended that you gather as much information as you can by reading other books, articles, papers, and essays, and by talking to as many people as you can about koi and all other aspects of keeping koi.

Conditioning Adult Koi

Healthy young start with healthy adults. That is why nutrition is so important. Koi are opportunistic feeders. That is, they will feed on basically anything that is edible. Some edibles are more nutritious than others, so it is important to feed your koi a good-quality diet with regular offerings of a variety of treats. For starters, a good-quality pellet food that is high in protein makes a perfect base or staple diet for your broodstock. The pellets do not have to be of a large size even though the adults may be huge. They should be large enough for the fish to easily pick them off the surface, though.

Adult koi will relish feedings of many other foods besides the pellets. Live and fresh foods offer a wide degree of vitamins and nutrients that may be lacking in commercial diets.

The feeding of any of the listed foods should be in moderation and only in addition to their staple diets. Many koi will develop favorite foods, and it is acceptable to feed these a little more frequently. However do not allow the diet to get one-sided because this will lead to nutrition problems and possibly health problems down the road.

Part 5

Some examples of live foods are:

- Earthworms
- Brine shrimp
- Mealworms
- Wax worms
- Crickets
- Minnows (yes, koi will readily consume small feeder fishes)
- Fresh foods can also encompass a variety of things, such as:
- Peas
- Hardboiled eggs (chopped of course)
- Dark green leafy vegetables
- Whole grain breads
- Oatmeal
- Crabmeat
- Diced shrimp

The conditioning process for adult broodstock should begin shortly after the winter dormancy period is completed. Bringing the adults out of dormancy is not particularly tricky but may be problematic if the wrong foods are offered. You should never bring a koi out of dormancy with rich, high-protein diets, as they can develop bloat disease and possibly die from it. Rather, bring them out from their long, winter rest with bland foods, such as wheat-germ-based diets. These are the same diets that should be fed to your koi during the autumn months as well. Once the adults are feeding normally, you can begin to switch them over to richer diets with heavy supplementation of higher protein and vitamin foods.

After several weeks of conditioning, your female koi will begin to show signs of ripening. The gravid females will become increasingly uncomfortable with their dilemma of holding all of those eggs (sometimes exceeding 20, 000) and will be looking for a place to deposit them. All of this occurs while the males of the pond are in heavy pursuit of her. She is now ready to spawn and will readily do so if she can find a suitable nesting site to release her eggs.

Spawning Sites

The female koi will readily seek out the best places of their home to deposit the eggs. Immediately after-ward, the male will deposit his milt over the eggs, and a very high percentage of the eggs will become fertilized. This process usually takes place among dense vegetation along the pond's edge. However, if there is an absence of vegetation, then you may have to intervene by adding a spawning mat to the pond.

Spawning mats provide a safe haven for eggs and fry to grow and develop.

Spawning mats are very useful pieces of equipment for those who wish to provide a spawning site for their koi but do not want the hassle and mess that accompanies live plants. The mats provide protection for the eggs and fry but do not takeup a tremendous amount of space. They also don't die like plants do. This is a bonus because, as we all know; when plants die they can make quite a mess and often require more attention than the fish.

If you do have plants, as many outdoor ponds do, then you will want to make sure that they are in top condition. Large koi will often topple planters in their eagerness to spawn and may even

Part 5

uproot and break plants that are secured in heavy planters. Both male and female koi are responsible for these behaviors, but the juvenile or non-breeding koi in the pond will do more damage rooting through the plants to eat the eggs. Koi are not very good parents. In fact, they are not even really considered to have any parental skills at all. They lay the eggs and forget about them or they lay the eggs then turn around and eat them. With behavior like this, it really makes you wonder how any survive at all.

Spawning mops are another useful piece of equipment when it comes to providing a suitable site for egg laying. Essentially, spawning mops are just long pieces of yarn or other material bunched together. To make your own spawning mop is very simple. First, take the desired type and amount of material and lay it out so as to form a long row. Next, find the center point and bend the material slightly to mark it. Now place a suitable sized rock (one that will effectively sink the mop) in the bend and wrap the material around the rock so the rock becomes a weight. This "weighted" side is the bottom of the mop. Twist the weighted end several times and tie it off using another, much shorter, piece of material, and your spawning mop is complete. Now you can place these almost anywhere in the pond, though koi seem to favor shallow water.

Common Problems

Breeding koi is not as easy as it may appear. There are a host of problems that you may encounter before, during, and after spawning takes place. There may not only be problems with the fish but also with the water, equipment, liner, and weather as well. Large-scale breeding of koi usually takes place in huge, outdoor mudponds. Mudponds are basically large pools of water that have no liner. They are also referred to as "earth ponds" because the water is always in direct contact with the soil.

Sorting and culling koi can be a long and arduous process.

Problems that occur before breeding season are most commonly associated with the failure to gather enough nutrients to develop eggs or milt. The period between winter dormancy and spring breeding is a stressful one for the fish's body. Koi are usually rather thin or slightly emaciated after winter, and if the water temperature climbs too fast, then their metabolism will also increase too fast. The affected fish will be unable to nourish their body fast enough to keep up with their metabolism, and they will succumb to malnutrition.

Chronic diseases, such as ICK or Fin Rot, will also decrease the chances for a successful spawning from the affected fish. These fish will be too stressed from dealing with the illness and will be unable to produce the right ingredients for spawning. The same is true if you have a high percentage of predators frequenting your pond.

Part 5

People with a high population of raccoons often report that their koi, even large ones, are reluctant to enter the shallows (probably for fear of being caught by a raccoon), and this is where the vast majority of spawning takes place.

The biggest problem that you will commonly encounter during spawning time is the males' relentlessly chasing the females. The only way to prevent such behavior, which is usually more stressful on us than the koi, is by separating the males and females. That is fine unless you really do want babies. If you do wish to have your koi breed, then you will most likely just have to grin and bear it.

There are times where enough is enough though, and then you must intervene or else you will be left with a dead koi. Overly aggressive males can beat up the females pretty badly, even to death, so if you see one or more males becoming increasing belligerent, then you may have to separate that male from the females. Try not to move the females; simply remove the male and place him in a covered holding container, such as a plastic clothes basket with floats attached to it, and let him sit in there for a few days. That is

Female koi will search tirelessly for a suitable spawning site.

usually enough to calm him down. Overly aggressive males may sometimes force a large female, or other males, to jump out of the pond. That is yet another good reason to intervene. There is nothing more painful in fishkeeping than to know that you could have done something about losing a particular fish.

Post-spawning activity is usually pretty dull and uneventful. One of the biggest problems that koi keepers may encounter is that some females did not spawn during the normal season. There may have been factors that you were unaware of, or it could be that the female was not ready when the males were. Whatever the reason, you now have a potential problem on your hands. Females that do not lay their eggs have one of three things happen to them: they may release the eggs regardless of the presence of a male, reabsorb the eggs into their own bodies or, in the worst case, become egg-bound. When a female becomes egg-bound, the eggs solidify into a solid mass, making it impossible to release them even if she wanted to.

Dealing with an egg-bound female koi can be very frustrating because there is little one can do in order to save her life. There are occasions where the fish will be able to loosen the mass so that it will break up and reabsorb into the female's body. However, these occasions are rare and should not be taken for granted, especially because they may require some work on your part.

First, and most importantly, do not remove the fish and try to squeeze the eggs out—you will kill the koi. You should also not

Part 5

remove the koi from the pond and attempt to massage the egg mass in order to help break them up. You may cause further damage, which can also lead to the death of the koi.

Instead, remove the female carefully from the pond and place her in a separate quarantine aquarium indoors or in a place where she can be observed. The water should be taken directly from the main pond so there will be no adjustments in the sense of chemistry needed. Use a good-quality filter and keep the tank dark, so the koi will not stress out too much. Over the next few days, do not feed her and slowly increase the water temperature a few degrees each day by using an aquarium heater. The absence of food and rise in water temperature will sometimes trigger a response to absorb any extra nutrients that the body has. Because she is still gravid, the body will hopefully attempt to reabsorb the unfertilized eggs. The body does not know that they are all bound together nor does it seem to care. After a few more days you can offer small amounts of food and note her response. Also pay very close attention to her belly. If the swelling decreases, then you have most likely succeeded in curing the egg binding.

Caring for Your Koi
Year Round

Koi require care and attention all year long. That means that on the hottest days and coldest nights, you should always have it in the back of your mind that your prized koi are out enduring the elements. They are totally at the mercy of your experience and the amount of time and planning that you put into your setup. The more

After a long winter, your koi will want to be fed.

planning that has gone into your koi pond, the better off your fish should be during foul weather. Often, new hobbyists have a tendency to forget about their koi when the weather turns gray. Ironically, the fouler the weather, the more attention the fish sometimes need.

In order to keep your koi and their environment as healthy as possible, each season warrants a different kind of care and maintenance.

Autumn

Many people assume that koi just sit on the bottom of the pond when the cooler temperatures start creeping in. The truth is that koi and other pondfishes do not usually just sit around when the cooler temperatures set in. During the fall season, the time period between winter dormancy and their active behaviors of the end of summer, koi are actually still active, even though temperatures may be cooler.

During autumn, you will want to remove as many leaves as you can from your pond's surface.

Autumn is best known for flocks of waterfowl and other birds migrating south to spend the winter months in warmer climates and for the leaves of deciduous trees turning brilliant colors of yellows, oranges, and reds. However, one behavior usually goes unnoticed. This is the feeding frenzy that many species of fish, and even reptiles, go through in order to ensure that they have enough body fat storages to last them until spring and the return of warmer temperatures.

Koi don't just turn themselves off simply because the air temperature dropped to 55 F the night before. They go through a slow process of turning off for the season. This process usually includes seeking out foods higher in proteins and sugars to help store fat and provide energy should the koi need it during an emergency, such as escaping from a bold raccoon or other predatory animals that may enjoy taking a dip in your pond in the off-season.

Water lettuce will die off in cooler months.

Koi may also be seen rooting through dead vegetation in your pond in search for uneaten insect larvae and for a suitable site to rest for the long winter ahead. Autumn is the time of year where large koi may congregate in small, tightly formed schools and cruise the pond together.

Part 5

This behavior is thought to occur because the drive to reproduce is turned off due to falling water temperatures and, more likely, the decrease in daylight hours.

Autumn is also the time of year when you should pay very close attention to sediment buildup in your pond. If dead leaves, branches, acorns, or pine cones are allowed to sit it your pond all winter, they will decay and can cause water chemistry problems that may be somewhat difficult to fix at a later date. If the buildup is thick, a layer of toxic hydrogen sulfide gas can accumulate, and when this layer is disrupted, it can cause a major die-off in your pond, due to the toxicity of the gas and it's effect on the pond's pH value. Therefore, make sure that you remove all dead plant matter before it has the chance to build up and cause major problems down the road.

Water hyacinth is a popular species of floating plant but needs to be removed in autumn.

Many people cover their ponds with netting to help prevent leaves and other matter from falling in. These nets are available at most pet shops, garden-supply stores, and home improvement centers.

Their cost is relative to the overall dimensions of the netting but is usually very affordable. Netting is also a good idea if you are having a constant problem with predators, especially birds, getting into your pond and eating your fish. Always be sure to use a surface-skimming net to help remove leaves that still get into your pond.

Smaller koi that may have reached sexual maturity over the summer months may try to get a quick spawning in from time –to time. These koi usually succeed in the spawn; however, the eggs may prove to be a tasty treat to the larger koi in the pond and provide a great dietary supplement to their menu just prior to the onset of winter. Sometimes, the male will eat the eggs as fast as the female lays them rather than fertilize them. If you witness this event, and the males devour the eggs right away, then you may want to re-examine their diet, as it may be lacking an important ingredient.

As the temperatures fall lower and lower, the amount of daylight hours will also decrease. This decrease in daylight is the primary reason for koi beginning their winter dormancy. Certainly temperature does play a role, but recent studies indicate that the amount of daylight is the real trigger. After all, there are plenty of cold days in the fall season that would have you thinking that it is winter already.

Winter

When people think of winter, they usually picture a landscape of snow-covered evergreens and holly bushes with small birds jumping

Part 5

Keep a hole in the ice for gas exchange.

through the branches. It is safe to assume that your koi see things differently, far differently. By the end of December in the northern states, the water temperature of your koi pond is usually in the low to mid 40s. Southern states are somewhat warmer, but unless you live in the deep South, chances are your water temperature is still pretty chilly. Now your koi are considered to be in their dormant stage due to the lack of regular movement and feeding. But being dormant is not the same as hibernation.

This is the time of year where people think that their koi just sit around and do nothing. Well, on gray overcast days that may be true; however, on those bright, sunny (freezing) days, it is not uncommon for your fish to slowly move around the pond. It is not as easy to observe this behavior in larger ponds, but in smaller ponds with fewer fish, it is quite a common sight. For this reason, you should keep at least one water pump running. It is preferred to keep the filter running as well, but for some reason, people have a tendency to turn it off. If your pond filter sits for more than a day without water running through it, the beneficial bacteria will die. That means that you will have to recycle your entire pond again in the spring. It is far easier and more beneficial to simply keep it on.

Only rarely will the fish rise to feed (it is not uncommon for them to not rise at all, however) and, unless it is unseasonably warm out or the water temperature has warmed up considerably, it is best to still withhold food during the winter months. If you feed your koi and they have not digested the food by nightfall, when the temperatures fall again, then there could be serious health problems or even death should the water temperature fall and the koi's metabolism decreases with a full belly. In all honesty, the only people who should

Koi may still rise to the surface occasionally in winter.

feed their fish during cooler weather are those who have installed heater/chiller units to maintain a more steady temperature or those who keep their koi indoors for the cooler weather.

Winter can prove to be fatal for your fish if you are not well informed and prepared for it. For example, never forcibly break the ice that forms on the pond's surface. This will cause a strong percussion and can damage your fish's inner ears or may even cause shock and, subsequently, death. Also, never do a large water change unless it is absolutely necessary. Even if you replace the pond's

Part 5

water with fresh cold water from your tab, chances are it will still be ten or more degrees warmer than the pond's water, as tap water is usually in the low 50s at its coolest.

The best thing you can do to keep your koi healthy and happy during winter months is to basically do everything that you would normally do except shy away from feeding and any major water changes. Certainly, it is acceptable to add a few gallons to top off your pond or you need to change a small volume of water to help stabilize your water chemistry as long as extremes are avoided.

Another good thing to do for your koi is to provide them with some type of shelter. These can be cinder blocks with large pieces of slate or shale bridging them together as to provide shelter. Large terracotta clay chimney flues can also be used to provide shelter. The flues come in an assortment of lengths and diameters but most commonly measure 16 inches long by 5 inches wide. The koi will usually sit in them when the weather gets really bad, such as during prolonged downpours or snowstorms.

Spring

The gray days of winter give way to the warm weather and clear skies that springtime brings. Koi and all other pond fish are most active during these months. Once the days become longer and the temperatures become warmer, your koi will begin to show signs of breeding. The telltale signs of this are increased swimming activity and a bulging of the abdomen.

In early spring, you should take a real good look around and in your pond. During this time, you can perform a water change and really do a thorough cleaning, being sure to remove any extra detritus from the pond's floor. You should also take a careful look at your fish's bodies and fins. Sometimes, parasites like anchor worms or fish lice will mysteriously show up. These parasites are introduced into the pond

Springtime is when many types of new life will emerge in and around your pond.

from other animals and can sometimes affect fishes when they are coming out of dormancy, while they're bodies are weak and hungry for nutrients.

By mid-spring you will see several species of plants beginning to sprout and trees beginning to blossom. The plants in your pond will begin to take up nutrients once again, and this will help to relieve your pond's waste –load, thus improving water quality. Spring is also when you may experience a somewhat heavy algae bloom in your pond. This can be discouraging and dangerous, but it is natural. Algae blooms actually occur each season throughout the year, but some are more drastic than others. The springtime algae bloom is the one most commonly seen, but it is usually less dangerous than those that sometimes occur during summer months.

Part 5

This is a koi owner's dream pond.

Feeding your koi during the spring is usually very easy. Often, they are downright starving from a long winter with no food. This leaves them hungry and sometimes even malnourished by the time spring rolls around. If your koi were improperly conditioned prior to winter, then there may be irreversible damage done to internal organs. This is why some koi die a few weeks after the weather breaks, even though they appear to be happy and healthy.

Springtime is also the season for insects to begin coming out and exploring your pond. Koi relish most species of common insects, such as houseflies, pill bugs, crickets, moths, and worms. Koi really love worms. Insects are a completely natural food item for your koi and will greedily take them off of the water's surface. Therefore, you should encourage the presence of most insects around your pond by not using insecticides.

Insecticides can cause a great deal of trouble in your pond by poisoning the water and, consequently, killing your koi and other pond fish. Any insects that are offered to your koi as food should be guaranteed not to contain any amount of insecticides. Even small quantities can be very harmful to any aquatic life in your fishpond.

Summer

Hot, long days and warm, humid nights are telltale signs that summertime is upon us. Koi and heat usually do not mix well, and you must be extra careful not to allow your pond to overheat during the summer. There are several ways to help prevent overheating your pond, and it is strongly recommended that you take

Greenwater can cause oxygen deficiency in ponds during summer months.

as many precautions as possible to ensure that your prized pets are not subjected to extraordinary temperatures.

One of the best things you can do in the preparation stage is to plan so that the pond is placed in an area where it receives no more than four to six hours of direct sunlight. This will help ensure that, even on the hottest days of summer, the intense sun will not beat down on the pond's surface all day. Also, the less direct sunlight the pond gets exposed to, the less of a chance of having an explosive algae bloom that, as you know, can cause major problems to your pond's overall well-being.

In well cared-for ponds, the koi usually exhibit ravenous appetites, consuming whatever they can find that is edible. However, if your

Part 5

Always pay careful attention to water chemistry during summer months.

pond is too warm, you may experience behavior that mirrors that of dormancy, the only difference being that the fish will circle just under the water's surface in an effort to get more oxygen. The main reason for this is that the water temperature is most likely too warm and there is not enough dissolved oxygen to allow the fish to act normally.

Water is not capable of holding a high level of dissolved oxygen at warmer temperatures, so you will be forced to provide a supplemental aeration device, such as a blower or large water fountain to force a constant supply of fresh oxygen into the water. Such equipment is costly, and the need for them could easily be avoided all together if the pond is planned out correctly from the beginning.

Another good way to help prevent overheating due to sunlight exposure is to plant trees in locations that will provide at least some relief from the sun. There are many risks involved in doing this, so you should consult your local landscaping professional or garden-pond center regarding these risks, but trees can come in handy, especially if they are in large planters aboveground. You must always be careful with trees that are in planters too, however, as they can fall over during strong storms with high winds. The branches are heavy, especially in the middle of the summer when they are covered with leaves. The branches can also be sharp and therefore are able to cause large tears or puncture wounds in the lining of the pond.

Bridges offer another fantastic opportunity to help provide shade for your pond and allow you to view your koi from above. As you are well

Bridges and docks make perfect observation points for large ponds.

aware of by now, koi are bred to look their best from above anyway. Bridges can be as elaborate or simple as your taste dictates. Very large ponds allow you to have a walkway to a small, covered gazebo situated somewhere in the middle of the pond's open-water areas. Other ponds allow you to have a simple dock that extends only a small distance into the pond. Either way, your choices for offering your fish shade can be as varied as the type of koi you have in your pond.

Another one of the biggest concerns for pondkeepers during summer months is the amount of vegetation that can grow in a pond. Submerged plants can become out –of control in a relatively short period of time. This can also cause a sudden decrease in dissolved oxygen during warm, summer nights. Always be careful to

Part 5

remove any plants that are not supposed to be there. Your pond is at its highest ecological diversity during summer months, but you have to remain focused on the health of your fish. Allowing your pond plants to grow uncontrollably is not a good example of proper pond care. Of course, submerged plants are really the only ones that will cause oxygen problems during the summer, however. Terrestrial and emergent plants will die and breakdown in cooler weather. Therefore, it is best to remove any of them that are not needed.

Final Thoughts

Koi are remarkable fish. They come in many colors and can exhibit dramatically long, flowing fins and a vast array of scalation. Most grow huge even by pondfish standards and are capable of outliving their owners. They are usually very hardy and disease-resistant, as long as proper water quality is maintained and they are fed a varied diet of high-quality foods. They need a lot of space, in order to reach their full potential, and powerful filters, in order to keep their ponds well balanced.

Aside from their care requirements and overall dimensions, koi are true pets. They are capable of owner recognition and will often "beg" for food when their favorite human approaches. In time and with good care, you may be able to reproduce your koi. This is the ultimate in satisfaction for many hobbyists because selling off some of your fish's offspring allows you to gain back some of the money that you initially sunk into your hobby and spread their genes to other hobbyists so they may benefit from your hard work.

Glossary

Aka Bekko

Red koi with black sanke-type markings

Aka Muji

Nonmetallic red koi

Aka sanke

Sanke-type with large areas of red

Bekko

Black sanke-type markings on white, red, or yellow

Doitsu

No scales on the body other than the enlarged scales that may run down the sides or on either side of the lateral line of the koi

Gin-Rin

Reflective silver scalation

Hanatsuki

A hi pattern that reaches the mouth

Hi

Red

Hi Showa

More than half the body is red when viewed from above

Hi Utsuri

Black koi with red markings

Higoi

Red colored koi

Hikarimoyo

A show class for all multicolored metallic koi except Showa and Utsuri

Kage

Black or dark reticulated marking over white

Kawarimono

A class for all nonmetallic koi not included in any other group

Ki

Yellow

Kigoi

Nonmetallic lemon-yellow koi

Kin-Gin-Rin

A koi with highly reflective silver or gold scalation

Kiwa

Border of red and white at the rear edge of hi patterns

Kohaku

White body with red markings

Kuchibeni

appearance of having lipstick or colored lips

Kumonryu

Black doitsu with small amount of white on fins, body, and head

Magoi

The ancestral black carp

Maruten

A self-contained red marking on the head while having isolated red markings elsewhere

Nidan

Two-step pattern

Ogon

Single-colored metallic koi

Orenji

Orange

Sandan

Three-step pattern

Sanke

White body with red and black markings

Shimi

Undesirable individual or areas

Shiro Bekko

A white koi with black sanke-type markings

Shiro Itsuri

Black koi with white markings

Shiro Muji

All white, nonmetallic koi

Showa

Black koi with red and white markings

Shusui

Doitsu Asagi

Sumi

Black

Tancho

Having a circular red marking on the head with no other red on the body

Utsurimono

Black koi having red, yellow, or white markings

Yondan

Four-step pattern

Resources

Tropical Fish Hobbyist

The leading aquarium keeping magazine, Tropical Fish Hobbyist has been the source of accurate, up-to-the minute, fascinating information on every facet of the aquarium hobby including freshwater fish, aquatic plants, marine aquaria, mini-reefs, and ponds for over 50 years. TFH will take you to new heights with its informative articles and stunning photos. With thousands of fish, plants, and other underwater creatures available, the hobbyist needs levelheaded advice about their care, maintenance, and breeding. TFH authors have the knowledge and experience to help make your aquarium sensational.

P.O. Box 427

Neptune, NJ 07754-9989

For subscription information please e-mail:

info@tfh.com

or call:

1-888-859-9034

Associated Koi Clubs of America

The AKCA is devoted to keeping and showing koi. They provide very useful pond information and publish the magazine Koi USA. To find a local club, please visit the website for information on over 100 affiliates.

KOI USA

P.O. Box 469070

Escondido, CA 92046-9547

For subscription information please e-mail:

www.akca.org

Water World

Water World is a company that specializes in koi ponds, fish, plants, as well as a full line of accessories. They also offer expert advice from professionals that have been in the business for many years. They are located at:

Water World at Monmouth Feed

294 Squankum Road

Farmingdale, NJ 07727

Or you can visit them on the web:

www.waterworldonline.com

Index

Photo Credits